THE OFFICIAL
JOHN WAYNE
BIG BOOK OF
DAD JOKES

JEREMY K. BROWN

FOREWORD

WHILE MOST PEOPLE REMEMBER JOHN WAYNE as the stoic cowboy who struck fear into the hearts of his foes, the man behind the big screen persona wasn't always so serious. In fact, when I think of my father, I often hear the sounds of his laughter first. Whether he was recalling amusing memories with his friends on the *Wild Goose*, cracking jokes with his co-stars between takes or lovingly teasing one of us kids, Duke loved to fill his life with laughs whenever possible.

Now, as you read these John Wayne-inspired jokes as well as anecdotes and quotes from his film career and personal life, my hope is that you and those close to you will be inspired to do the same. Whether you choose to tell them to your own children or grandchildren or keep them to yourself for when you need a good guffaw, you'll be carrying on Duke's legacy of laughter. Because even though his job required him to keep a stiff upper lip, he was still a dad at the end of the day. And he had the jokes to prove it.

—Ethan Wayne

CONTENTS

Duke laughs with his son Patrick Wayne.

JOKE SECTIONS

12
JOKES ON THE RANGE

Quips about cowboys
sure to crack up
the corral.

42
GENERAL HUMOR

Military zingers
worthy of a salute.

68
CINEMATIC JOKES

Wisecracks inspired by a variety
of John Wayne films.

102
SHAGGY DOG STORIES

Long-form jokes, long-lasting laughs.

136
A FEW FOR THE ROAD

A handful of stray jokes you'll be
glad you stuck around for.

FEATURES

08
BONDED BY MISCHIEF
The amusing antics of
John Wayne and Ward Bond.

38
TURNING THE TABLES
How Duke got the last laugh on
The Harvard Lampoon.

84
GOOFIN' BETWEEN TAKES
Stories of John Wayne's good-
natured gags behind the scenes.

130
SIDE-SPLITTING SCENES
A roundup of Duke's funniest
moments in classic films.

154
SMALL SCREEN, BIG LAUGHS
John Wayne's variety TV show
appearances were always a hoot.

170
KIDDIN' THE KIDS
Duke's children share stories about
their father's humor.

FUNNY FILMS

32
McLINTOCK!
A comedy about a couple quarelling
for all the town to enjoy.

64
THE QUIET MAN
An amusing classic highlighting the
humorous nature of Irish in-laws.

96
NORTH TO ALASKA
A gold miner hires a prostitute to
mend his friend's broken heart.

110
DONOVAN'S REEF
A veteran runs a beloved bar where
friendly brawls become tradition.

Lucille Ball
and John Wayne
on *The Lucy
Show*, c. 1966.

"YOU KNOW WHAT I THINK AGES [ACTORS]? STAYING UP ALL NIGHT WATCHING THEIR OLD MOVIES ON TELEVISION."

—*The Lucy Show*

John Wayne and Ward Bond on the set of their 1956 film *The Searchers*.

BONDED BY MISCHIEF

DUKE'S FRIENDSHIP WITH WARD BOND WAS FULL OF GOOD-NATURED GAGS AND ROWDY SHENANIGANS THAT MOST WOULD ONLY DREAM OF ENGAGING IN.

G iven the way their lives intersected, John Wayne and Ward Bond seemed destined to become the best of friends. The experience of rising through the ranks of Hollywood made Duke and Bond incredibly close, as the two went from working as extras to leading men over the course of 23 shared films. John Wayne's career would of course ascend to unimaginable heights over the years, and Bond stuck by the star not for a ride on his coattails, but for the incredible friendship they shared. And that friendship was largely built on the pair's penchant for busting each other's chops.

Duke first met Ward Bond when the two were teammates on the gridiron at the University of Southern California. And though the young Duke's time as a Trojan at USC would be cut short unexpectedly, the setback did not spell the end for his connection to Bond. The two first wound up sharing a film set as extras in a flood scene for Michael Curtiz's 1928 film *Noah's Ark*. Soon after, while under the wing of John Ford as a propman and occasional extra, Duke provided the director with a group of extras for the 1929 film *Salute* by calling in his former teammates, including Bond. From that point on, the two friends continued to climb the Hollywood ladder, becoming closer—and more off-kilter—friends in the process.

As their star statuses grew, the two pals soon became just as well known for their shared irreverence as their work on the silver screen. John Wayne loved to joke to anyone who knew Bond that his fellow former football player earned the nickname "The Judge" at USC because of how often he was sitting on the bench. And director John Ford, while known for being a firm filmmaker and guiding mentor to the star, was always eager to join the legend in poking fun at Bond. Whenever the troublemaking trio worked on a film together, Duke and the director had their own inside joke, of which Bond was the butt—literally. During filming, Ford would often sneak close-up shots of Bond's ample posterior, generating a surefire source of laughs when looking at dailies later on. The joke would eventually reach a new level of affectionate mockery when Ford and John Wayne were off shooting 1950's *Rio Grande* on location in Utah without Bond on set. Teasing their absent buddy from a distance, the star and the director mailed Bond a photo of a horse's rear end captioned, "Thinking of you."

While John Wayne and Ward Bond forged much of their friendship through good-natured verbal jabs, they were also just as likely to dish out actual fisticuffs. On one occasion, Bond bet Duke that even if both men were standing on a piece of newspaper, the latter wouldn't be able to punch him. Duke took the wager, and Bond—in a moment of inspired strategy—took the newspaper and laid it in a doorframe, then closed the door, shutting off the other side. Duke casually took his place on the paper, then punched Bond in the face through the door. During a particularly rowdy visit to the Hollywood Athletic Club, Bond threw a cue ball at Duke, who ducked as the flying object went crashing through a glass window and struck a passing car. Fortunately for all involved, the driver of the vehicle was thrilled to find the incident was caused by two major movie stars.

The two men's friendly physicality became such a staple that by the time John Wayne and John Ford made their last film together, 1963's *Donovan's Reef,* the director found a way to immortalize the unique existed between Duke and Ward Bond. When he was struck by a car shortly before John Wayne's wedding, Bond summoned the same type of grit his friend was known for and showed up on crutches to perform his best man duties. And in 1960, following Bond's untimely death, John Wayne delivered a moving eulogy at his longtime pal's funeral, saying, "We were the

"We were the closest of friends, from school right on through…. He was a wonderful, generous, big-hearted man."

aspect of their relationship. In the film, Duke's Patrick "Guns" Donovan and Lee Marvin's Thomas "Boats" Gilhooley engage in a just-for-fun knock-down, drag-out fist fight as part of an annual tradition. Though John Wayne and Ward Bond never had such a tradition, it likely wouldn't have surprised anyone who knew them if they decided to schedule their fights rather than start them spontaneously.

Through all of their practical joking and horseplay, a companionship as true as any always closest of friends, from school right on through…. He was a wonderful, generous, big-hearted man."

Even after his passing, Bond managed to get the last laugh with an act of "generosity." In his will, he left John Wayne the shotgun that Duke, years earlier, had borrowed on a hunting trip and accidentally used to shoot Bond in the backside. The gesture was a testament to the strength of their friendship—no matter how many bumps or bruises they ended up with, they could always laugh it off.

JOKES
ON THE RANGE

John Wayne on the set of *The War Wagon* (1967).

THEY'RE SO FUNNY YOU'LL FALL OFF YOUR HORSE!

A COWBOY bursts into the office of the local architect.

"Quick! Quick!" he says. "I need you to help me draw up a new plan for the town."

"What are you talkin' about?" the architect asks.

The cowboy says, "I'm trying to get out of having to duel Black Bart, and he says this town ain't big enough for the both of us!"

A COWBOY walks into a saloon and sits down to play poker.

"I'm sure glad to be playin' with folks in town again," he says. "Spent the last few weeks playin' up at a camp in the mountains."

"What was the problem with that?" asks the dealer.

"This is much more relaxing. The games at camp were always *in tents*."

A SHERIFF is standing on a hill, guns drawn, observing the notorious Rusty Spurs gang in the valley below. Once his deputy arrives with reinforcements, they'll ride down and arrest the ne'er-do-wells.

Just then, he hears his deputy riding up behind him with a cat under his arm.

"No, no, NO!!" yells the sheriff.

"What's wrong?" asks the deputy.

The sheriff angrily points to the cat. "I told you to bring a *posse*!!"

JOKES ON THE RANGE

A COWBOY rides into town and sees an angry mob gathered around the gallows with pitchforks and torches. Standing on the gallows, arms bound, is a man wearing rather strange clothes that the cowboy can't quite make out.

"What's going on?" he asks a preacher in the mob.

"That there's Leafy Dan," the preacher tells him. "His pants are made of leaves. His shirt's made of leaves. His boots, his belt, even his hat, all made of leaves."

"So they're hangin' him for his fashion choices?" asks the cowboy.

"No," says the preacher. "They're hangin' him for *rustling.*"

A COWPOKE goes to the doctor's office with the seat burned out of his jeans. The doctor looks at him in disgust.

"Were you sittin' on the stove again?" asks the doctor.

"Yessir," sighs the cowpoke.

The doctor shakes his head. "How many times have I told you? That's not how you ride the *range!*"

HAVE YOU HEARD of the famous cowboy actor who did all his movies with a broken leg?

Splint *Eastwood*

DID YOU HEAR about the cowboy who needed to borrow money?

His horse had to give him a few bucks.

DID YOU HEAR about the cowboy who held up the acting teacher?

He wanted to rob a stage coach.

WHY DID the cowboy take his pony to the doctor?

He noticed he was a little horse.

WHY DID the cowboy jump up when he sat on his boots?

Something spurred *him on.*

WHAT DOES a cowboy get when he rounds up 18 cows?

20 cows

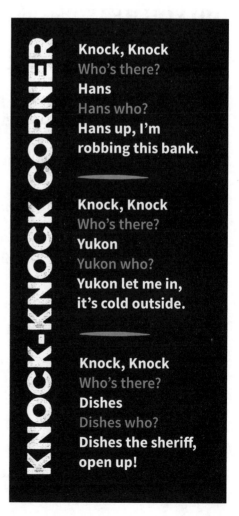

KNOCK-KNOCK CORNER

Knock, Knock
Who's there?
Hans
Hans who?
Hans up, I'm robbing this bank.

Knock, Knock
Who's there?
Yukon
Yukon who?
Yukon let me in, it's cold outside.

Knock, Knock
Who's there?
Dishes
Dishes who?
Dishes the sheriff, open up!

JOKES ON THE RANGE

WHY DID the cowboy's horse want to quit his job?
He was saddled with too much responsibility.

WHY DID the cowboy get a new horse?
His old one was too much of a neigh sayer.

DID YOU HEAR the story about the cowboy trying to get his horse to stop?
It was a real tale of whoa.

DID YOU HEAR about the cowboy whose biggest fans were horses?
He had a real colt following.

WHY DID the cowboy always tell jokes to his cows?
To turn them into a laughing stock

WHY DID the rancher move all his cows to the second floor of the ranch?
He liked to raise the steaks.

WHAT DID the father horse say to his son when he wanted to marry young?

"Wise men say only foals *rush in...."*

A RANCHER was showing a young ranch hand around when they came to a pen with two-legged cows propped against the fence.

"What do you call these?" the ranch hand asked.

"Lean beef."

"And what about those?" the hand asked, pointing to a group of no-legged cows. The rancher smiled.

"Those are my ground beef."

JOKES ON THE RANGE

WHY DID the cowboy not tell any cow jokes?
He knew he'd butcher them.

WHY DID the rancher refuse a shipment
of male cows?
He knew it was just a load of bull.

WHY DID the cowboy flunk out of art school?
He could only draw pistols.

WHAT DID the cowboy say to the cactus?
"You're looking sharp!"

THE SHERIFF walks into a saloon and hears the
bartender calling out "Sarsaparilla! Make it a double!!
Another round!!!"

"Hold on there partner!" says the sheriff. "In this town, I
call the shots."

WHAT DOES a cowboy get when he has a stomach bug?
Dia-yee-haw

DID YOU HEAR about the cowboy who worked at the glue factory?
He stuck to his guns.

WHY DID the rancher's cows seek therapy?
They felt seen, but not herd.

WHAT DID the rancher say to the cows after they stayed up too late?
"It's pasture *bed time...."*

WHERE DID the rancher's cows lose all their money?
At the cowsino

HOW DID the cow feel when she couldn't give any milk?
Like an udder *failure*

WHY DID Roy get a corduroy vest, a corduroy shirt, corduroy pants and a corduroy hat?
He wanted to feel like a full Roy.

JOKES ON THE RANGE

WHAT DID the cowboy hat say to the neckerchief?
"You hang around here. I'll go on ahead."

WHICH COWBOY in the corral wears
the biggest hat?
The one with the biggest head!

A RATTLESNAKE walks into a saloon.
The bartender says, "How'd you do that?"

TWO COWBOYS are riding through the desert when
they hear the sound of war drums thumping in the
distance. One cowboy looks at the other.
"I don't like the sound of those drums."
The other cowboy shrugs and says, "Maybe he just needs
to warm up."

WHAT DID the cowboy say to the off-key fiddler?
I don't like your tone, mister.

A COWBOY rides into town with flies buzzing all around him.

"Tarnation!" says a passerby. "You ever shoo those things?"

"Naw," says the cowboy. "I just let 'em go barefoot."

John Wayne on the set of *The War Wagon* (1967).

JOKES ON THE RANGE

WHERE DO mediocre singing cowboys go?
The O.K. Chorale

WHAT DID the cowboy say to the governor as he was about to be hung?
"Howdy, pardoner*!"*

WHAT DOES a cowboy call the list of horses he wants to ride?
His buck it *list*

A COWBOY is riding along the range, when he comes across another cowboy lying down with his ear to the ground. He gets off his horse and walks over to him, and the other cowboy says, "Herd of buffalo, about 20 or 30... then a covered wagon with a family heading west."

"That's amazing!" says that cowboy. "You can tell all that just by listening to the ground?"

"No," the other cowboy says. "They ran over me about a half hour ago."

WHAT DO rich cows drive?
Cattle-*acs*

WHY DID the dog challenge the cowboy to a duel?
He shot his paw.

A DEPUTY rides into town. The sheriff says to him, "What took you so long?"

The deputy points to the arrow sticking out of his horse's rear.

"Sorry," he says. *"Injun trouble."*

A HORSE walks into a restaurant.

The waiter says, "Hey!"

The horse says, "How did you know?"

WHEN IS a cowboy's dinner not hot?
When he has chili

WHAT DO you call it when a cowboy comes back to life?
Reintarnation

KNOCK-KNOCK CORNER

Knock Knock
Who's there?
Wanda
Wanda who?
Wanda see what you're up to today!

Knock Knock
Who's there?
Cows go
Cows go who?
No, that's owls, cows go moo!

Knock Knock
Who's there?
Justin
Justin who?
Justin town, thought I'd say hi!

JOKES ON THE RANGE

WHAT WAS the hardest part of the bow-legged cowboy's job?
Keeping his calves together

DID YOU HEAR about the cowboy who brushed his teeth with gunpowder?
He shot his mouth off.

WHY WAS the lasso stressed out?
It was tied in knots.

WHY WERE the rancher's chickens so tired?
They were working around the cluck.

WHAT DOES a horse use to make its sandwiches?
Thoroughbread

A PROSPECTOR walks into a saloon.
The bartender says, "Sorry, we don't serve miners."

John Wayne and Maureen O'Hara on the set of *Big Jake* (1971).

WHAT HAPPENED to the cowboy who stood behind his horse?

He got a kick out of it.

A COWBOY went up to a rancher and asked how much for his cattle.

"$100 a head," said the rancher.

"Great," said the cowboy. "How much for a whole cow?"

JOKES ON THE RANGE

DID YOU HEAR about the most difficult horse on the ranch?

He liked to stirrup *trouble.*

WHY DID one horse marry the other?

He was looking for a stable relationship.

WHY DID the cowboy fire his pistol in the air?

He wanted to shoot the breeze.

WHY WAS the horse embarrassed at the stable?

Because he didn't change Jockeys *for months.*

WHY WAS the cowboy looking for paper towels?

He was a Bounty hunter.

A COWBOY walks into a saloon and sits down at the bar and starts complaining.

"My feet hurt from my boots, my hat is too small, my horse doesn't like me..."

Before he can go on, the bartender holds up a hand.

"Sorry, pardner," he says. "We don't have a *whine* cellar."

WHY DID the cowboy wash his clothes after holding up the stagecoach?
He wanted to make a clean getaway.

DID YOU HEAR about the cowboy who had to stop offering bull rides?
Business kept falling off

WHERE DOES a rancher get to know his cattle?
At a meat-and-greet

WHY DID the gunslinger shoot the clock in the town square?
He had time to kill.

WHY DID the cowboy roll around in the grass when he got dirty?
It was scrub *grass.*

JOKES ON THE RANGE

A COWBOY walks into a saloon and sees a bunch of men and a dog playing poker.

"That's the most incredible thing I've ever seen," said the cowboy, pointing to the dog.

"Not really," said the bartender. "Every time he gets a good hand he wags his tail."

WHY DIDN'T the cowboy want to hear any more cow jokes?

He'd herd *them all before.*

DID YOU HEAR about the cowboy who was bitten by a cow?

It just grazed *him.*

WHY DID the cowboy stop robbing trains?

It was too hard to keep track.

DID YOU HEAR about the cows who overthrew the rancher?

They staged a moo-tiny.

WHY DID the rancher wear tights and a mask?
He was a professional rustler.

WHY WAS the executioner not good at his job?
He never got the hang *of it.*

WHAT DO gold prospectors eat at their camp?
Karat cake

John Wayne on the set of *The Alamo* (1960).

JOKES ON THE RANGE

WHAT IS the first thing a sheriff does when investigating a train robbery?
Establish a loco-motive

WHY DID the cowboy sign up for lasso lessons?
He got roped into it.

WHAT DID the cactus say to the cowboy?
"Let's stick together."

WHY DID the cowboy quit the rodeo?
The pay was terri-bull.

WHO'S the oldest sheriff in the West?
Wyatt AARP

AFTER a long ride across the desert, a cowboy walks into a saloon and sits at the bar. Next to him, another cowboy looks down at a bowl of chowder. "Hey partner," the first cowboy says. "Are you gonna eat that?" The other cowboy gives him a strange look, but passes the bowl over. Ravenous from his ride, the first cowboy digs in. He gets about halfway through when he sees a dead mouse in the bowl. Horrified, he throws up all the chowder into the bowl. "Ayuh," the other cowboy says. "That's about as far as I got, too."

A COWBOY was riding across the desert after being lost for weeks. He sees another cowboy riding up to him.

"How's it going?" the other cowboy says.

The first cowboy sighs and says, "Long time, *no sea*."

THE SHERIFF is walking through the streets of town, when he comes across a cowboy lying face-down in the street and groaning.

"Alright, mister," says the sheriff, hauling the cowboy to his feet. "Where are you from?"

The cowboy points up. "The balcony."

John Wayne and Maureen O'Hara on the set of the 1963 film *McLintock!*

FUNNY FILM

McLINTOCK!

DUKE'S 1963 FAMILY AFFAIR IS A RIOTOUS REMINDER OF THE WESTERN GENRE'S COMEDIC POTENTIAL.

With the arrival of the 1960s, John Wayne officially entered the elder statesman era of his Hollywood career. Even though the Western icon known for his blazing guns and flying fists was now 56 years old, that didn't mean he had to slow down. Instead, Duke embraced this new status by taking on more family-focused projects, even involving his own kin when possible. With his 1963 comedy-Western classic *McLintock!*, the actor got to share the screen with his son Patrick while his eldest son Michael produced the film under the family's Batjac banner, together creating a rollicking 127 minutes filled with quotable quips and uproarious action.

The film stars John Wayne as the titular rich rancher George Washington "G.W." McLintock, who has plenty on his plate between the farmers, government workers and land-grabbers at odds with each other in hopes of getting a piece of his territory. Even more conflict comes McLintock's way, however, when his estranged wife Katherine (Maureen O'Hara) arrives in town demanding a divorce as well as custody of their daughter Becky (Stefanie Powers). In one of the comedy's most inspired slapstick scenes, McLintock is able to achieve a bit of catharsis when he quickly shifts from peace-maker to punch-thrower. After an earlier incident with a shotgun-wielding local, Duke's rancher tells the troublemaker, "Pilgrim, you caused a lot of trouble this morning, might've got somebody killed—and somebody ought to belt you in the mouth! But I won't, I won't.... The hell I won't!" before jabbing the man in the jaw and sending him barreling down the hill and into a mud pond. This causes the surrounding onlookers to erupt into an all-out brawl in a scene that's just as humorous as it is thrilling. As the men slug it out and slide through the mud, even Katherine McLintock lets her frustrations fly with the mud as she removes a quill from her hat and plants it into a man's posterior.

Having previously perfected their chemistry in the likes of *Rio Grande* (1950) and *The Quiet Man* (1952), John Wayne and Maureen O'Hara were able to take their talents as the bickering on-screen couple to the next level for *McLintock!* After McLintock tells his wife he saw a picture in the newspaper of her dancing with the governor, Katherine replies, "At least he's a gentleman." Not allowing her to get the last laugh, McLintock scoffs, "You have to be a man first before you're a gentleman. He misses on both counts."

Later, when McLintock's employee Drago (Chill Wills) suggests Katherine's elevated status has extinguished her usual kindness, she asks the rancher, "Are you going to stand there with that stupid look on your face while the hired help insults your wife?" Not one to miss such an opportunity, McLintock retorts, "He doesn't know any better than to tell the truth. And I can't help this stupid look. I started acquiring it as you gained in social prominence!"

Beyond McLintock and Katherine, the family feuding between the rancher and his daughter is also played for laughs. Feeling wildly disrespected by her boyfriend Devlin's (Patrick Wayne) opinions on women who indulge

The knee-slapping success of *McLintock!* made it clear John Wayne's family business was in very capable hands. In its assessment of the film, *Time* magazine gave praise that could be applied to not only Duke, but also his talented sons, writing, "It is dedicated to the

"YOU HAVE TO BE A MAN FIRST BEFORE YOU'RE A GENTLEMAN. HE MISSES ON BOTH COUNTS."

their desires before marriage, Becky McLintock insists her father shoot the unapologetic man. "If you're my father, if you love me...." she provokes. Grabbing a gun, McLintock declares, "I'm your father, and I sure love ya!" before blasting Devlin in the stomach. As Becky screams in shock, McLintock reveals he used a race pistol with a blank cartridge in an amusing meta moment wherein Duke pseudo-shoots his real-life son in the name of fatherly love.

proposition that where there's a will, there's a Wayne." And noting the incomparable chemistry the legend shared with his co-star, *The New York Times* wrote, "When it comes to sparring partner for Mr. Wayne in a battle of the sexes, no one has ever approached the vigor of the titian-haired Maureen O'Hara." With his friends and family on board, John Wayne was able to craft a laugh-filled film that fans continue to enjoy with their own pals and kin today.

**John Wayne and
Bob Hope on
*The Bob Hope
Special* c. 1971.**

"YOU THINK I WALK FUNNY, YOU SHOULD SEE MY HORSE— HE'S WEARING A CORRECTIVE SADDLE."

—With Bob Hope at the 26 Bar Ranch

John Wayne takes questions at Harvard University with a student dressed as his character Rooster Cogburn.

TURNING THE TABLES

THANKS TO THE UNSHAKEABLE GOOD SPIRITS OF DUKE, A SARCASTIC "HONOR" PRESENTED BY THE STUDENTS OF HARVARD UNIVERSITY TURNED INTO FUN FOR ALL INVOLVED.

Among the many qualities for which he was known, there were two things you could always count on from John Wayne: he would never back down from a challenge and he would unapologetically be his genuine self at all times. Late in his life, the legend got the chance to remind everyone just who he was in a fairly unlikely setting: the campus of Harvard University. As the Vietnam War was still raging on, the notably liberal institution hosted Hollywood's most famous conservative in hopes of having some one-sided fun at his expense. But in true Duke fashion, what could have been a hostile exchange between two opposing ideologies turned out to be a day full of laughs enjoyed by both sides of the political divide.

39

TURNING THE TABLES

John Wayne's visit to the home of the Crimson came about thanks to a cheeky challenge presented by the president of *The Harvard Lampoon*, eventual *Saturday Night Live* writer James Downey. In his letter to Duke, Downey wrote: "You're not so tough. You've never pored through dozens of critical volumes on imagist poetry....You've never had to do three papers and a midterm all for one course." Realizing the university's satirical (and famously left-leaning) paper was looking to take aim at his macho persona and likely his conservative views, John Wayne penned a response that previewed the witty rebuttals he would soon deliver in person: "I'm sorry to note in your challenge that there is a weakness in your breeding, but there is a ray of hope in the fact that you are conscious of it."

The challenge accepted, Duke arrived in Cambridge, Massachusetts, on January 15, 1974, ready to accept a satirical "Man of the Year" accolade from *The Harvard Lampoon*. Though beloved *Columbo* star Peter Falk was the actual recipient of Harvard's 1974 "Man of the Year" award, the icon wasn't about to turn down an opportunity to creatively make the Ivy Leaguers the butt of their own joke. Rather than showing up in a limousine as almost any other star of his status would, John Wayne instead leaned into the student body's perception of him as a staunchly conservative patriot and rode down Massachusetts Avenue atop an M-113 Armored Personnel Carrier tank operated by 5th Cavalry reservists. With gamesome guns blazing, he then partook in the annual ceremony's preliminary parade, furthering the pomp and circumstance his arrival established.

Once John Wayne took the stage for a press conference inside the filled-to-capacity Harvard Square theater, the real fun began. The actor fielded questions from the eager attendees, most of whom were aiming to poke fun at his image and pin him down for his political viewpoints. One student reporter in attendance snidely asked Duke if he looked at himself as an "American legend." Taking the sarcastic inquiry in stride, the actor replied, "Well, not being a Harvard man, I don't look at myself any more than necessary." When the question "What do you think of Women's Liberation?" was pointedly posed, the legend again seized the opportunity to turn the baited query into a setup for a purposefully dated punchline. "I think Women's Lib is fine as long as they're home by six to cook my dinner," the star responded, drawing big laughs from the crowd.

Further proving himself a good sport, John Wayne didn't shy is what you've been eating over at The Harvard Club."

Despite the whole day being built around a faux honor intended to mock the man, John Wayne—as he had against tougher odds in less agreeable circumstances— emerged from the Harvard ceremony victorious. Through his signature charm and quick-witted responses, the actor was not only able to win over the crowd, he also

"WELL, NOT BEING A HARVARD MAN, I DON'T LOOK AT MYSELF ANY MORE THAN NECESSARY."

away from poking fun at himself, particularly on the subject of his physical appearance. Boldly addressing the toupee Duke was indeed sporting at the time, one student asked, "Is that hair real?" "It's real..." the icon began. "It's not mine, but it's real."

Another audience member cracked wise asking, "Is it true that since you've lost weight your horse's hernia has cleared up?" to which John Wayne responded, "Well, the weight was too much for him so we canned him, which showed them how much more enjoyable the event could be as a good-natured two-way roast. Ultimately, the willingness to take a joke demonstrated by both sides proved to be a winning formula, bridging a gap between the two otherwise disparate entities. Rather than argue politics, they put it all aside in favor of forging a fun memory. The event serves as a reminder of a universal truth Duke always held dear: no matter who we are, we all love to have a good laugh.

41

General
HUMOR

John Wayne in
*Cast a Giant
Shadow* (1966).

FACE FRONT AND
BRACE FOR LAUGHTER!

~ARMY JOKES~

TEN HUT! TIME TO FALL IN FOR A PLATOON FULL OF JOKES THAT ARE SURE TO MAKE YOU SALUTE.

WHAT'S sweaty and smelly and carries a rifle?
A foot *soldier*

DID YOU HEAR about the soldier who spilled ice cream on patrol?
He was charged with desserting *his post.*

HOW IS an army recruit like a computer?
You need to punch information into both of them.

WHAT'S a new recruit's least favorite month?
March

WHY was the private court-martialed for running over a bag of popcorn?
Because of all the kernels *he crushed.*

GENERAL HUMOR

WHERE DO kids who join the army go?
The infant-ry

WHY DID the soldier wear a t-shirt to battle?
It was a casual-tee *of war.*

A YOUNG BOY is walking down the street and sees a veteran walking toward him with a cane.
"Thank you for your service," the boy says. "Were you shot in the army?"
"No," says the veteran. "In the leggy."

WHY DIDN'T the soldier go to war after putting on his uniform?
He was too fatigued.

WHY WAS the T-Rex contracted by the military?
He was a small-arms dealer.

WHAT DO army chefs always have in the mess hall?
A salt-*rifle and* pepper *spray*

WHAT HAPPENED when the marching band accidentally walked over the officer?

They had a flat major.

A YOUNG MAN shows up at the recruiting station.

"What's the lowest rank in the Army?" he asks.

The recruiter says, "It's private."

The recruit frowns and says, "Come on, you can tell me."

AS THE Commander-in-Chief, where does the President keep his armies?

In his sleevies

WHY DID the army attack Turkey?

Because it was Thanksgiving.

WHY DID the soldier desert his post to use the latrine?

He put doody *before honor.*

KNOCK-KNOCK CORNER

Knock Knock
Who's there?
Dora
Dora who?
Dora bell's broken, that's why I knocked.

Knock Knock
Who's there?
Spell
Spell who?
OK, that's easy, w-h-o.

Knock Knock
Who's there?
Déjà
Déjà who?
No, déjà vu is how it's pronounced!

GENERAL HUMOR

HOW DID the soldier feel after surviving both mustard gas and pepper spray attacks?
Like a seasoned veteran

WHY DID William quit the army?
He was tired of the Sergeants telling the troops to fire at will.

WHAT DO you call a soldier charged with watching the latrine?
A loo tenant

MY GRANDFATHER was in charge of editing Hitler's correspondence.
He was a real *Grammar Nazi!*

~NAVY JOKES~

ANCHORS AWEIGH! HERE'S A BOATLOAD OF FUNNIES THAT WILL KEEL HAUL YOU RIGHT OVER THE EDGE.

A SEAMAN reports for duty on his first day on an aircraft carrier. He's feeling nervous so he approaches another sailor.
"Do big ships like this sink often?" he asks.
"No," the sailor says. "Just once."

WHY DIDN'T the sailor want to talk about his time in the lifeboat?
It was a real oar deal.

WHAT vegetables do they never serve on a naval ship?
Leeks

WHERE DOES a sailor keep his sports equipment?
In Davy Jones's locker

WHAT DO you call a sailor who lives in the Arctic and eats fish?
A Navy seal

WHY DID the sailor go to the rear of the ship?
He was given a stern order.

DID YOU HEAR about the sailor who drowned opening a window?
Yes, him and everyone else on the submarine.

GENERAL HUMOR

WHY DIDN'T the sailor get off the boat?
He didn't want to give in to pier *pressure.*

WHAT HAPPENED when the red destroyer crashed into the blue destroyer?
All the sailors were marooned.

WHAT HAPPENED to the sailor who crashed his ship?
He had to go to anchor management.

I HEARD that the Icelandic Navy now has barcodes on their ships.
It's so they can Scan-da-navy-in.

DURING the Cold War, where did Soviet pirates come from?
The USS-Arrrrr

DID YOU HEAR the new Iraqi Navy now has glass-bottomed boats?
It's so they can see the old Iraqi Navy.

John Wayne (second from left) on the set of *They Were Expendable* (1945).

A HUSBAND and wife are out to dinner, when suddenly the husband clutches his chest and falls forward.

"Help!" the woman yells. "My husband is having a heart attack!"

A man rushes over to attend to the man and says, "Don't worry, ma'am, I'm a Naval surgeon."

"No no," cries the woman. "It's his heart, not his belly button!"

WHY DID the submarine business fail?

It went under.

GENERAL HUMOR

WHERE DO sailors take their ship when it's sick?
To the doc

A SAILOR on watch was wondering why another ship was sailing too close to his ship.
Then it hit him.

A GROUP OF sailors were lost at sea after their ship sank. After three days, another boat came on the horizon and pulled up alongside them.

"Thank goodness!" one sailor said. "We're so glad to see you. We've been lost for three days."

"Don't get too excited, sailor," said a man in the other boat. "We've been lost for three weeks."

~AIR FORCE JOKES~
TRY AND STAY BELOW THE HARD DECK AND DON'T REACH FOR THE EJECTOR SEAT AS THESE LAUGHERS REACH NEW HEIGHTS!

WHAT DO plane propellers have in common with fans?
When they turn off, people start sweating.

HOW DID the airman like his job building planes?
He found it riveting.

WHY DIDN'T the pilot offer excuses for being late for duty?
He knew they wouldn't fly.

WHY COULDN'T the two pilots talk while on patrol?
They couldn't break the sound barrier.

RIGHT BEFORE he was about to be discharged, an Air Force pilot sat down with his commanding officer.

"Well," says the officer. "What did you think of your time in the Air Force?"

The pilot smiles. "It had its ups and downs."

WHY DID the pilot quit the Air Force?
His career didn't take off.

DID YOU HEAR the joke about the F-16 fighter jet?
Eh, it'd probably go over your head.

HOW DO pilots get clean?
Jet wash

GENERAL HUMOR

WHY DID the pilot get reported to the ASPCA?
He got caught dogfighting.

MY FATHER personally brought down more than 50 planes.
He was the worst mechanic in the Air Force.

WHY DO parachutes have a perfect operational record?
If one doesn't work, you never hear the user complain.

WHY'S IT so hard for Air Force pilots to concentrate?
Their heads are always in the clouds.

AN AIR FORCE pilot is flying over enemy territory, when a voice comes over the radio to deliver a message.
"Get off the radio!" the

KNOCK-KNOCK CORNER

Knock Knock
Who's there?
Beef
Beef who?
Beef friendly and open the door!

———

Knock Knock
Who's there?
Rufus
Rufus who?
Rufus leaking, better come out here!

———

Knock Knock
Who's there?
Gus
Gus who?
No need to guess, I know who!

pilot says. "This is a secure channel, you moron!"

"Do you know who this is?" says the voice. "This is Colonel Johnson!"

"Do you know who this is?" asks the pilot.

"I certainly do not!" says the Colonel.

"Well, then so long, moron!"

WHY DIDN'T the pilot like to fly over enemy territory?
He always got flak *for it.*

WHY DID the buck join the Air Force?
He wanted to be a bombar-deer.

WHY WASN'T the pilot good at golf?
He was always getting bogeys.

WHY WASN'T the pilot allowed to fly?
He had a bad altitude.

HOW DOES an Air Force pilot like his pizza?
"Plane."

GENERAL HUMOR

WHY DIDN'T the pilot tell jokes during missions?
They didn't always land.

DID YOU HEAR about the pilot who flew more than 100 missions in the same plane?
He was very dedicated to his craft.

WHAT BRANCH of the military is exclusively for rabbits?
The Hare *Force*

~MARINES JOKES~

FROM THE HALLS OF MONTEZUMA, TO THE SHORES OF TRIPOLI, THESE JOKES ARE SURE TO BRING A SMILE TO EVEN THE MOST STOIC JARHEAD.

WHAT DO you call a bad Marine?
Rotten to the corps

A MARINE goes on deployment and promises to write his girlfriend a letter every day. Six months later, he gets a phone call from her.
"I'm getting married!" she says.
"To who?" the Marine asks, in shock.
"The mailman!"

WHY DID the recruit flunk out of boot camp?
He was a sub-Marine.

WHAT DO you call the best players in the Marine Corps Band?
The top brass

WHAT HAPPENED to the Marine who ate too many burritos before morning calisthenics?
He had a dishonorable discharge.

DURING basic training, the new recruits were tired of having to deal with their drill sergeant, who made every day miserable.

One day, he got in the face of a young recruit. "Son," he said. "Someday I'll be dead and then you can go ahead and spit on my grave."

"No sir," said the recruit. "After I leave the Marines, I'm never standing in line again!"

DID YOU HEAR about the barber who wanted to be a Marine?
He made the cut.

GENERAL HUMOR

A YOUNG MAN goes to a recruiting station.

"What branch are you thinking of?" asks the recruiter.

"I don't know," the young man says. "Maybe the Army?"

"The Army?" asks the recruiter. "Son, do you know what 'Army' stands for?"

The young man said he didn't.

"Ain't Ready to be a Marine Yet!"

WHAT BRANCH of the military do zombies join?

The Marine Corpse

HOW DO you know when you meet a Marine?

Don't worry, he'll tell you.

WHY DON'T Marines go bald?

Even their hairline doesn't retreat.

A PRIVATE meets up with his platoon. The next morning, they head out to battle, and the sergeant is not impressed with his performance.

"Private!" the sergeant says. "Did you come here to die?"

"Sir, no sir!" says the private. "I got here yesterday!"

Director Mervyn LeRoy and John Wayne on the set of *Without Reservations* (1946).

WHAT DO you say to a demolitions expert when you don't want to hear their opinion anymore?
"OK, Boomer"

WHAT DOES a Marine study before he gets married?
The rules of engagement

DID YOU HEAR about the high-ranking Marine who didn't have a lot of detailed information?
He just had General *knowledge.*

GENERAL HUMOR

WHERE DO the branches of the armed services come from?
The mili-tree

WHAT DID the Marines' social media manager say when he was outnumbered?
"Retweet!"

~CAVALRY JOKES~
HEAR THAT BUGLE BLAST? IT'S TIME TO CHARGE HEADLONG INTO LAUGHTER!

WHAT DO you call a confederate soldier who bombs at standup comedy?
A rebel without applause

DID THE South enjoy jokes during the Civil War?
General Lee *not*

WHAT DO you call a replica of a calvary rider's weapon?
A carbine *copy*

WHAT DO you call a cavalry with no horses?
Free of charge

DURING the 1860s, what did the North and the South eat their food with?

Civil wear

HOW DID the cavalry soldier end up soaking wet while patrolling the fort?

He just couldn't see that well.

A GROUP of cavalry soldiers were riding through the plains, when a scout rode up with his head bandaged and his uniform torn.

"Sir!" he said to the general. "I have good news and bad news. The bad news is we are completely surrounded and a thousand braves are going to ride us down and slaughter us by sunset."

"My word!" said the general. "What could be the good news?"

"We won't have to ride back through Nebraska again!"

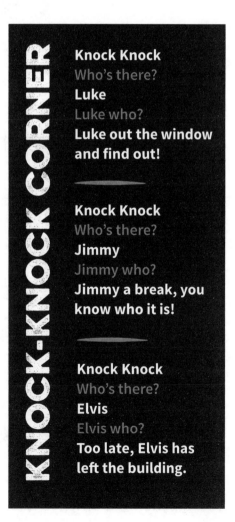

KNOCK-KNOCK CORNER

Knock Knock
Who's there?
Luke
Luke who?
Luke out the window and find out!

Knock Knock
Who's there?
Jimmy
Jimmy who?
Jimmy a break, you know who it is!

Knock Knock
Who's there?
Elvis
Elvis who?
Too late, Elvis has left the building.

GENERAL HUMOR

WHY DIDN'T Ferris play reveille for the soldiers, as he usually did?
  It was Ferris Bugler's day off.

WHY DID the cavalry soldier stop using a sword?
  There was no point.

WHERE CAN cavalry riders take their horses when they get sick?
  A horse-spital

WHAT HAPPENED to the cavalry soldiers when the horses broke into the barracks after lights out?
  They all had night mares.

WHAT DID the cavalry call themselves after they went on a diet?
  The light *brigade*

WHY DID the horse quit the cavalry?
  He needed something a little more stable.

George O'Brien and John Wayne on the set of *She Wore a Yellow Ribbon* (1949).

WHAT DID the designer think of the cavalry horse's gear?

He thought it was too tacky.

DID YOU see the cavalry instructor's new book?

It's called How to Train Your Dragoon.

WHY WAS IT so easy to pick up the calvary rider's sword?

It was a light saber.

John Wayne with his son Ethan and *Wild Goose* captain Bert Minshall.

"ALWAYS SPIT ON NEW SHOES FOR GOOD LUCK."

—Told to *Wild Goose* captain Bert Minshall,
after spitting toward Minshall's new deck shoes

John Wayne and
Maureen O'Hara
in *The Quiet Man*
(1952).

FUNNY FILM

THE QUIET MAN

DUKE AND HIS PALS JOHN FORD AND MAUREEN O'HARA CREATED A COMEDY BRIMMING WITH IRISHNESS THAT REMAINS A MERRY GOOD TIME TODAY.

In 1952, John Wayne fans flocked to theaters to see the actor as Sean Thornton in *The Quiet Man*, a unique role that would take Duke out of the blistering West and place him in a sleepy Irish village. But while the setting is serene and the protagonist is a pacifist, the film is far from a quiet affair.

THE QUIET MAN

Featuring scenes poking fun at Irish tropes, dialogue that cracks wise about the unholy matrimony of love and money and a climax that earns hearty laughs, the film remains a riotous standout in the legend's vast filmography.

After accidentally killing a man in the ring, prizefighter Sean Thornton returns to his birthplace, the Irish village of Inisfree, where he vows to live the rest of his life peacefully. Hoping to settle into his family's old cottage, Thornton immediately draws the ire of townsman "Red" Will Danaher (Victor McLaglen), who'd already had his eyes on the home. Inadvertently taking the conflict between the two to an even more personal level, Thornton soon meets and falls in love with a woman named Mary Kate (Maureen O'Hara), who happens to be the antagonizing man's sister. Undeterred by Danaher's threats, Thornton goes through with acquiring the cottage. Additionally, he also makes his move on Mary Kate, leading to one of the film's most memorable, amusing moments.

When Thornton finally makes his intentions known by pulling Mary Kate in for a passionate kiss, she responds with an attempted slap, blocked by Thornton, and exclaims: "It's a bold one you are! Who gave you leave to be kissing me?" The scene not only cemented the perfectly blended comedic romance the iconic co-stars became known for, it also proved O'Hara's grit. While filming a take, the actress fractured a bone in her hand when Duke blocked her slap. But because the film was shot out of order, she couldn't wear a cast and had to tough it out for the remainder of shooting. This, as well as many more rugged qualities she would display in their years to come, would cause John Wayne to later dub O'Hara "the greatest guy I ever knew."

But while Mary Kate is quick to attempt a strike, Thornton remains steadfast in his refusal to lift his fists—that is until Danaher takes a swing at him first. After Thornton exposes Danaher's cruel objection to his sister's marriage in front of the whole town, he adds literal fuel to the fire by tossing the previously withheld dowry into a kiln, revealing that the money never mattered. Finally, with tensions boiling over, the two soon-to-be brothers-in-law throw fists in a sprawling fight as onlookers drop what they're doing to place bets. As the slapstick brawl rages all over town, a comedic camaraderie begins to bloom between the men. After a jab to the jaw sends him barreling into the river, of John Ford, John Wayne and Maureen O'Hara worked together, it provided plenty of proof that the co-stars and director were a movie-making trifecta. *Life Magazine* showered the film with praise, particularly for its winning depiction of life on the Emerald Isle, writing: "[It] foams like a glass of Guinness with all the

"SHOULD GO DOWN IN HISTORY AS ONE OF THE GREATEST COMEDIES EVER MADE." —*LOOK MAGAZINE*

a soaking wet Danaher asks Thornton if he's had enough. "No!" Thornton shouts, to which Danaher replies, "Well, give a man a hand then!" A few blows later, Danaher insists he's "as fresh as a daisy." "You look more like a Black-eyed Susan to me," Thornton quips. Eventually, the brawlers land in a pub where they naturally become chummy and call a truce over a couple of hard-earned pints.

Though *The Quiet Man* was only the second time the trio classic attributes of the Irish: their brogue, hot tempers, passing for betting, above all, their belligerence, which keeps them whacking at each other in a bloodthirsty and utterly charming way for the two hours of film time." *Look Magazine*, meanwhile, made a bold proclamation that, as far as Duke's fans are concerned, turned out to be prophetic: "Should go down in history as one of the greatest comedies ever made."

67

CINEMATIC
JOKES

John Wayne and Victor McLaglen in *The Quiet Man* (1952).

ALRIGHT, PILGRIM. HERE'S A BEVY OF ONE-LINERS AND PUNS INSPIRED BY SOME OF DUKE'S MOST FAMOUS FLICKS!

~THE QUIET MAN~

MUCH LIKE THE FILM'S LEADING MAN, THESE JOKES PACK A PUNCH, AND A TOUCH OF THE EMERALD ISLE.

WHAT did the one-eyed Irishman say when asked if he could still see?
"Eye!"

WHAT do you call a cubic zirconia in Ireland?
A sham rock

WHAT is a boxer's favorite part of a joke?
The punch *line!*

A BOXER goes to see his doctor because he's having trouble sleeping.
"Have you tried counting sheep?" the doctor asks.
"I tried," the boxer explains, "but every time I get to nine I stand up."

WHAT do you call boxers who can't last in the ring?
Briefs

CINEMATIC JOKES

WHY shouldn't you use an iron on a four-leafed clover?
You never want to press your luck.

A BOXER goes to visit his priest and says "Forgive me Father for I have sinned." The priest says, "What is it you wish to confess?" "I punched a man," says the boxer. "Beat him senseless. Didn't stop until he was unconscious on the ground." The priest says, "Well that's part of your profession. You've done nothing wrong." The boxer sighs and says, "No, Father, this was on the way here."

DID YOU hear about the boxers' union?
They demanded equal rights. And lefts. And uppercuts.

Maureen O'Hara and John Wayne in *The Quiet Man* (1952).

WHY shouldn't you make fun of an Irishman's last name?
Because it's O'ffensive.

WHAT DID the leprechaun say when he introduced himself to the genie?
I-rish

~ *HATARI!* ~
CATCHING SOME BELLY LAUGHS AND WILD ANIMALS IN EQUAL MEASURE.

WHERE do animals go when they lose their tails?
To a re-tailer

WHAT'S a traditional lion's greeting to tourists on safari?
"Pleased to eat *you!"*

WHAT DO you call a hippo with no eye?
A "HPPO"

CINEMATIC JOKES

WHY WAS the giraffe the favorite animal on the plain?
He stuck his neck out for everyone.

WHAT DID the hippo leave behind when he trampled the safari camp?
A hippo-pot-a-mess

WHAT TIME is it when a lion jumps into your truck?
Time to get out of the truck

WHAT DOES a snake do when it gets mad?
Throws a hissy fit

WHAT KIND of an animal sneaks off the plains without telling his wife?
A cheetah

WHY ARE leopards so bad at hide and seek?
They can't help but get spotted.

WHY ARE pandas so hard to reason with?
Everything is black and white to them.

A BEAR was interviewing for a job, but he didn't get it. Why not?
He was over-koala-fied.

~HELLFIGHTERS~
Turn up the heat with these fiery gut-busters.

WHY DID the arsonist get off Tinder?
He couldn't find any matches.

WHY DIDN'T the fireman respond to the call?
He got cold feet.

WHY DID the fireman need a vacation?
He was getting burned out.

WHY DON'T firemen post on message boards?
Too many flame wars

CINEMATIC JOKES

HOW DID the fireman feel about his job?
It was a love-heat *relationship.*

WHAT DID the house say to the arsonist?
"Look, but don't torch*!"*

WHAT HAPPENED when a fire broke out at the piano factory?
It was a case of musical chars.

WHY WAS the firefighter so upset when the shoe factory burned down?
He couldn't get over how many soles *were lost.*

WHY WAS the firefighter uncertain about starting a new relationship?
He'd been burned too many times.

MY GRANDPAPPY always used to say, "You've got to fight fire with fire."
It's why he lost his job at the fire department.

John Wayne and Ann Dvorak in *Flame of Barbary Coast* (1945).

~FLAME OF BARBARY COAST~

NO NEED TO GAMBLE—THESE JOKES ARE A SUREFIRE BET.

HOW DO you become a millionaire by gambling?
Start by being a billionaire

A MAN went to see his psychiatrist about his gambling problem.

"Tell me, doc," he said. "Is there a cure?"

The doctor just shook her head and said, "No dice!"

John Wayne and
Glen Campbell
on *The Glen Campbell
Goodtime Hour*,
c. 1971.

"I GUESS I'VE MADE OVER 200 [FILMS]... AND I'M GONNA KEEP ON MAKING 'EM UNTIL I MAKE ONE RIGHT!"

—On *The Glen Campbell Goodtime Hour*

CINEMATIC JOKES

WHY DID the poker player throw out his cards?
He just couldn't deal *with them anymore.*

A WOMAN comes running into her house, yelling and cheering.

"Pack your bags," she tells her husband. "I just won big at the tables!"

"Oh great!" the husband says. "Should I pack for warm weather or cold?"

"I don't care," says the wife. "Just be out by noon!"

HOW DO you make 50 ladies curse in church?
Yell "Bingo!"

DID YOU KNOW the Dalai Lama was a big gambler?
He likes Tibet.

WHAT DID the zombie do when he didn't have any dice at the craps table?
He just rolled his eyes.

WHY DON'T you ever see vampires at a poker table?
They can't handle the stakes.

WHY ARE British casinos so good for weight loss?
You can lose hundreds of pounds a day.

WHY DID the Englishman bring a mackerel to the poker table?
He wanted fish and chips.

~IDOL OF THE CROWDS~
ANYONE WHO DOESN'T LAUGH AT THESE JOKES WILL BE SPENDING SOME TIME IN THE PENALTY BOX.

WHERE DOES the majority of a hockey player's salary come from?
The tooth fairy

WHY DO Canadians go to the fights?
Because occasionally a hockey game breaks out.

A LOCAL hockey team lost their Zamboni driver.
They hope he resurfaces soon.

CINEMATIC JOKES

A HOCKEY COACH was watching his team practice and shaking his head at how terrible they were. Just then, the owner came over.

"We're trying to come up with a new name for the team," the owner said. "Any ideas?"

"How about the *Titanic*?"

"The *Titanic*?" said the owner. "Why?"

"Because both look good until they hit the ice!"

DID YOU hear what happened to the world's worst hockey team?

They drowned during spring training.

WHY WAS the carpenter such a lousy hockey player?

He kept getting nailed to the boards.

WHY DIDN'T the hockey player take cash?

He preferred a check.

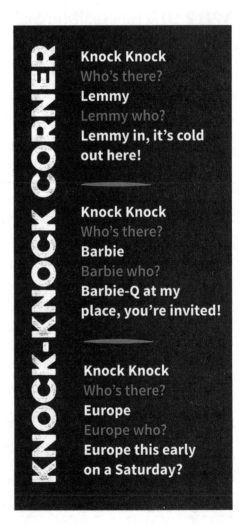

KNOCK-KNOCK CORNER

Knock Knock
Who's there?
Lemmy
Lemmy who?
Lemmy in, it's cold out here!

Knock Knock
Who's there?
Barbie
Barbie who?
Barbie-Q at my place, you're invited!

Knock Knock
Who's there?
Europe
Europe who?
Europe this early on a Saturday?

WHY DID the hipster watch swimming?
He was into hockey before it was cool.

DID YOU know hockey players are famous for their summer teeth?
Summer *in their mouths,* summer *on the ice*

~ *CALIFORNIA, STRAIGHT AHEAD!* ~
A COLLECTION OF SHORT JOKES FOR THE LONG HAUL.

WHAT HAPPENED to the trucker who fell asleep beside his muffler?
He woke up exhausted.

WHAT HAPPENED when the Smuckers truck crashed?
A massive traffic jam

A TRUCK DRIVER was eating at a roadside diner, when another trucker sat down next to him and handed him a $10 bill.
The trucker looked at the money and asked, "What's the *10 for,* good buddy?"

CINEMATIC JOKES

WHAT DO truckers like most about the movies?
The trailers

HOW DID the reporter end up getting hit by an ice cream truck?
He was looking for an exclusive scoop.

WHY DID the truck driver get out of the sanitation business?
He felt like his whole life was a waste.

DID YOU HEAR about the traffic jam of all the trucks delivering nachos?
Talk about a cheesy pickup line!

DID YOU HEAR about the country singer who got a self-driving vehicle?
His truck left him too.

WHAT HAPPENED when the cold medicine truck crashed?
There was surprisingly little congestion.

HOW DID the garbage truck driver fare with no training?
He picked it up as he went along.

~THE DROP KICK~
HIT THE GRIDIRON WITH A PACK OF JOKES THAT'LL HIT YOU LIKE A LINEBACKER.

WHY DID the lineman tackle the vending machine?
To get the quarter back

WHY DID the punter decide to retire?
He didn't get a kick out of his work anymore.

WHY IS IT hard for the NFL to hire female referees?
They'll throw flags for penalties you committed five years ago.

WHAT'S a dog's favorite play?
The flea flicker

WHY IS IT always so windy at MetLife Stadium?
Because of all the Giant fans in the stands!

Angie Dickinson and John Wayne on the set of the 1959 film *Rio Bravo*.

GOOFIN' BETWEEN TAKES

HE HAD A WELL-EARNED REPUTATION FOR BEING A CONSUMMATE PROFESSIONAL ON SET, BUT JOHN WAYNE NEVER MISSED AN OPPORTUNITY TO CRACK WISE WITH HIS COWORKERS WHEN THE CAMERAS WEREN'T ROLLING.

While being a revered Hollywood star is of course a dream job for many, the process of shooting a film can be draining for even the most passionate actors. For John Wayne, making a movie meant more than a chance to flex his acting muscles and craft another classic—it was an opportunity to spend quality time with his coworkers, many of whom he considered friends. And whenever some levity was needed on a long day, Duke was always willing to light up the set with hearty laughter.

In the spare moments on set in which he wasn't called upon to intimidate outlaws or leap fences on horseback, John Wayne could often be found bonding with the cast and crew over a game of chess or cards. It was during these moments where his comfort and closeness with his coworkers really took shape, naturally allowing his humorous instincts to take over. On the set of his safari film *Hatari!* (1962), the icon was able to turn a potentially terrifying situation into something straight out of a sitcom. After a day of shooting on location in Africa, Duke and his costar Red Buttons were playing a game of cards outside their tents when a wild leopard emerged from the shadows and came creeping toward them. Completely at ease with the situation, John Wayne simply quipped to his pal, "Buttons, see what he wants."

Duke's affinity for humor and hijinks on set can be traced back to his earliest days in Hollywood when he met the man who inspired the "John Wayne" persona, Yakima Canutt. The up-and-coming actor was first introduced to Canutt, who was hired to serve as his stunt double, on the set of the 1932 crime serial *The Shadow of the Eagle*. Shortly after meeting the man who would soon have a lasting impact on his career, Duke was told by fellow actor Bud

Osborne that Canutt's true role on set was to serve as a secret spy for one of the producers. Committed to convincing John Wayne the joke was legitimate, Canutt would follow the star of the serial around the set making notes of his every move in a notebook. Eventually, Duke got tired of being spied on, or so he thought, and nearly went after his stunt double. When Osborne revealed it was all a ruse, John Wayne found the whole thing hilarious and formed a fondness for his would-be shadow.

When he wasn't on the receiving end of a prank, Duke still had no qualms about appearing foolish for the sake of morale on set. In a biography, the legend's *Red River Range* (1938) co-star Lorna Gray (who later changed her name to Adrian Booth) recalled how John Wayne improvised a slapstick bit to boost spirits in more ways than one. While filming a scene in which John Wayne's Stony Brooke and Gray's Jane Mason are walking across a porch and down a flight of stairs, Duke kept stumbling over something, requiring the camera crew to reset and attempt to capture the scene again. Revealing the blooper was intentional, John Wayne whispered to his costar, "I'm going to stumble over a nail. Then I'm going to do it a couple more times. Pay no attention." As it turns out, the extras on set were just five minutes shy of earning overtime pay, and Duke was tripping over a nail intentionally to run out the clock. The gesture was generous, to be sure, but Duke's amusing method for stalling was also a testament to his comedic nature.

"I said, 'Is that what you want? OK,' and he walked away and turned around and said, 'That is...if you can.' So boy, we went at it!"

Later in his career, good-natured quarrels would become the foundation of one of John Wayne's most contentious coworker friendships: that with Dennis Hopper. During production for *True Grit* (1969), if current

---

WHEN HE WASN'T ON THE RECEIVING END OF A PRANK, DUKE STILL HAD NO QUALMS ABOUT APPEARING FOOLISH FOR THE SAKE OF MORALE ON SET.

Occasionally, Duke and his scene partners would even turn the job of acting itself into a gag. Describing their sibling-like relationship, Maureen O'Hara once recalled how the two tried to steal scenes from each other on the set of *The Quiet Man* (1952). After she turned in a respectfully understated take, Duke asked his co-star why she was holding back, to which she replied she was "playing half and half." "'To hell with that, you try to get it, you try to steal it,'" O'Hara remembered John Wayne insisting.

events were grinding his gears, the conservative Duke would jokingly aim the blame at the liberal Hopper. "If anything went wrong on set, he'd yell, 'Where's that pinko Hopper?'" the *Easy Rider* star remembered in an interview with *GQ*. "But he was always funny to me, I think he liked me." And despite the teasing Hopper received, the feeling was mutual. "*True Grit* was a pleasure," the actor told *InContention.com* in 2008. "He was the Duke, and I loved working with him."

Dean Martin and
John Wayne at
the 23rd Golden
Globe Awards.

"I ALSO WANT TO THANK DEANO FOR LEAVING HIS NEW YEAR'S EVE PARTY TO COME OVER HERE."

—Accepting the Cecil B. DeMille Award (presented by Dean Martin) at the 23rd Golden Globe Awards ceremony on February 28, 1966

CINEMATIC JOKES

WHAT HAPPENS to football players when they start to lose their eyesight?

They become referees.

HOW DOES the announcer kick off a game featuring the NFL's worst team?

"Let's get ready to fumble*!!!"*

WHAT'S the difference between a lousy football team and a dollar bill?

You can still get four quarters out of a dollar bill.

WHY DID the football player leave his glasses in the locker room?

He heard it was a contact *sport.*

DID YOU HEAR about the prison that wanted to stage a game between the NFL and the inmates?

It had its pros and cons.

John Wayne and Richard Attenborough on the set of *Brannigan* (1975).

~BRANNIGAN~

BRACE YOURSELF FOR A RIDE-ALONG WITH A SQUAD OF JOKES SO FUNNY IT'S CRIMINAL.

WHY DID the cops arrest the artist?
They thought he seemed sketchy.

WHAT HAPPENED to the cop who sneezed in bed?
He blew his cover.

WHY DID the cops have to cancel their yearly play?
They didn't have any leads.

CINEMATIC JOKES

DID YOU HEAR that all the toilets were stolen at the police station?
The detectives have nothing to go on.

WHAT HAPPENED when the cops raided a beehive?
It turned into a sting operation.

WHY DID the cop interrogate the orange?
He wanted to squeeze *him for information.*

WHAT HAPPENED to the cops who found their car up on blocks?
They worked tirelessly *to find the thieves.*

DID YOU HEAR about the robbery at the soap factory?
The thieves made a clean getaway.

WHAT ARE the best cops to have around when there are flies in the house?
The SWAT *team*

~HAUNTED GOLD~

A COLLECTION OF SPOOKY JOKES
THAT'LL MAKE YOU LAUGH YOURSELF TO AN EARLY GRAVE.

WHY DID the ghost get arrested?
For haunting *without a license*

HOW CAN you tell a ghost is lying?
You can see right through him.

WHY DIDN'T the ghost ride the roller coaster?
He didn't have the guts.

WHERE'S the best spot to see ghosts in the suburbs?
On a dead-end street

WHY DIDN'T the ghost ever go out in the rain?
It dampened his spirits.

DID YOU HEAR about the librarian who died when a pile of books fell on him?
His ghost had only his shelf *to blame.*

CINEMATIC JOKES

WHAT DID the ghost do when he needed a plus-one for a party?

He had to dig up an old friend.

DID YOU HEAR about the ghost who used too much starch in his sheet?

He was scared stiff.

~NORTH TO ALASKA~
THERE MAY NOT BE GOLD IN THEM THAR HILLS, BUT THERE SURE ARE PLENTY OF LAUGHS!

WHY was the miner depressed?

He couldn't see a light at the end of the tunnel.

WHAT key was the piano in when it fell down the mine shaft?

A flat miner!

A POLICEMAN stops a prospector and asks him, "Who's horse is this? Where are you going? What do you do for a living?"

The prospector smiles and says, "Mine."

WHY DID the miner quit his job?
Most of it was boring.

DID YOU HEAR about the guy who tried to be a prospector?
It didn't pan out.

DID YOU HEAR about the miner who started a company?
He wanted to mine *his own business.*

DID YOU HEAR about the miner who fell down the shaft?
His career hit rock bottom.

I HEARD there was a cave-in at the mine!
It was a miner *inconvenience.*

DID YOU HEAR about the prospectors who started playing baseball together?
It's just a miner *league team.*

John Wayne in a scene from *North to Alaska* (1960).

NORTH TO ALASKA

DUKE'S 1960 FILM ABOUT A PROSPECTOR CAUGHT UP IN AN UNLIKELY LOVE TRIANGLE STILL PACKS A POWERFUL COMEDIC PUNCH.

John Wayne characters are widely admired for being straight-shooters who rarely hesitate to speak their minds. In the Henry Hathaway-helmed 1960 film *North to Alaska*, marriage is on the mind of Duke's gruff prospector Sam McCord—and he frequently claims to want no part of it. Also on Sam's mind is a woman, however, and for the majority of the film, he does bite his tongue when it comes to his feelings for her. Along the way, *North to Alaska* provides plenty of laughs via its characters' cavalier approach to the complicated circumstances they face.

In the Alaskan city of Nome, Sam and his mining partner George Pratt (Stewart Granger) have struck gold. As George puts the finishing touches on the honeymoon cabin he's been building for his fiancée Jenny (Lilyan Chauvin), Sam travels to Seattle to bring his partner's bride-to-be to Nome—only to find that she's moved on and married another man. Wondering how he'll break the news, Sam hires "Angel" a.k.a. Michelle (Capucine), a prostitute, to soften the blow. But though Michelle is brought to The Last Frontier to help heal George's heartbreak, she quickly develops feelings for the emotionally closed-off Sam, who dodges any expression of reciprocal affection.

The true gold mine of *North to Alaska* is the dialogue, particularly when Sam counteracts Michelle's sweetness with his stubborn and acerbic anti-marriage remarks. While Sam is discussing his intentions to try to get George's life back on track, Michelle claims he's not making any sense and might be "too drunk to talk." "That's perfect, you even sound like a wife!" Sam replies. Michelle rejects the notion, saying she doesn't consider that a compliment, to which Sam agrees: "I'm on your side, lady!" Later, when trying to cheer up his brokenhearted buddy, Sam points to what he believes is a benefit of their setting: "George, a wonderful thing about Alaska is that matrimony hasn't hit up here yet. Let's keep it a free country!" Proving she's plenty capable of quips herself, Michelle even hits back at Sam with the occasional zinger. As the prospector is telling her George is at their gold site dealing with violent claim-jumpers, he remarks the dangerous situation might be good for his partner, saying, "One good thing about that, them shootin' at him will take George's mind off Jenny." "Yes," Michelle snidely replies. "A bullet through the head is always the best cure for love."

In addition to its knee-slap inducing dialogue, the film is also packed with plenty of slapstick humor. When a bar brawl breaks out early in the film, George socks the bartender in the nose, prompting a honking horn sound effect. Moments later, when Sam is caught by the sideswipe of a flying fist, he reacts by going cross-eyed and then tipping over backward, stiff and slow up the critics. In its November 9, 1960 review, *Variety* called the film "A good-humored, old-fashioned, no-holds-barred, all-stops-out Northern...the sort of easy-going, slap-happy entertainment that doesn't come around so often anymore in films," with specific praise for

---

"GEORGE, A WONDERFUL THING ABOUT ALASKA IS THAT MATRIMONY HASN'T HIT UP HERE YET. LET'S KEEP IT A FREE COUNTRY!"

---

like a hickory tree falling in the forest. And when it's Duke's turn to dish out the fisticuffs, he of course caps off the moments with some signature wit. In one scene, as Michelle is being bothered by a drunken logger, Sam simply walks up, drops the man with one punch and hands her a coffee. "Wasn't that man a friend of yours?" Michelle asks. "Sure," Sam replies. "Still is—or will be when he sobers up."

Upon its release, *North to Alaska* succeeded in cracking Duke's approach to the often-comedic role, adding, "Wayne displays a genuine flair for the lighthearted approach." Soon after, *The New York Times* dubbed the film "pleasantly boisterous," crediting the charismatic star with driving it to success, stating, "the proceedings are easily dominated by the indefatigable Mr. Wayne." Today, the film remains a guaranteed good time thanks to its timeless humor and endearing characters.

Duke and
his younger
brother Robert.

"MY NAME WAS MARION MICHAEL MORRISON, YOU THINK I FOUGHT? YES!"

—When asked on *The Phil Donahue Show* if he got in fights as a kid

Shaggy Dog Stories

John Wayne on the set of *Blood Alley* (1955).

Pull up a chair, pilgrim. These jokes take a little longer, but the laughter is worth waiting for!

JOE WAS experiencing a run of bad luck. He'd lost his job, gambled away his savings, his car had been repossessed and his wife had recently left him. Feeling depressed, he goes for a walk on the beach to rethink his life. As he's walking, he notices something tumbling over and over in the waves. He looks closer and sees it's a magic lamp straight out of *Aladdin*. Figuring he has nothing to lose, he picks the lamp up and rubs it. "Poof!" a genie comes out. He bows to Joe.

"Thank you for freeing me from the lamp, O great one," the genie says. "In exchange, I will grant you one wish."

"That's easy!" says Joe. "I want to be rich!!"

The genie nods his head.

"Your wish has been granted," says the genie. "Pleasure to meet you, *Rich*."

A HUSBAND AND WIFE are overjoyed when they finally have a baby boy. He is as happy and healthy as can be except for one problem—he does not talk. Not a word. Years go by and he says nothing. They take him to doctors. He says nothing. They take him to therapists. He says nothing. They take him to hypnotists. He says nothing. Eventually, after exhausting all their resources and trying everything with no luck, the couple assume their son will be mute the rest of his life. Then one day, when the boy is about 6, the family is eating dinner and the boy spits out his Brussels sprouts and says in a loud, clear voice, "Good Lord, these Brussels sprouts are the absolute worst thing I have ever eaten!!" The parents are overjoyed, running to their son and hugging him.

"You can talk! You can talk!" says his mother.

"Of course I can talk," says the boy.

"Then why haven't you?" asks the father.

"Because until now everything was fine!"

A MAN goes to pick up his newly-tailored suit and finds one arm is too short, one leg is too long and the neck is too wide.

"It's not a problem," says the tailor. "Just crook your arm at the elbow and hold it up over your head. And bend your leg at the knee until the pant legs line up. And for your neck, scrunch your shoulders up until your head is almost in the collar. Then it will fit perfectly!"

The man is displeased, but he does what the tailor suggests. So there he is, walking down the street with his arm crooked at a ridiculous angle and held up over his head, his knee bent and his body hunched and his shoulders up almost as high as his neck. He lumbers past an elderly couple on a park bench.

"Oh dear," says the old woman. "That poor man. He must be ill."

"Yeah, it's really sad," says her husband. "But look at the fit on that suit!"

A DUCK walks into a hardware store, waddles up to the counter and says, "Do you have any grapes?"

The man behind the counter says, "Look around you! This is a hardware store! No, we don't have any grapes!"

The duck leaves, but comes back the next day. Again, he asks, "Do you have any grapes?"

The man is annoyed and tells the duck, "Listen buddy, we don't sell grapes here. We sell hardware, so again, we don't have any grapes!"

The duck leaves and comes back the next day and for a third time, he asks, "Do you have any grapes?"

Now the man has had it. "OK," he says, "listen up. We don't have any grapes, we never had any grapes and we never will have any grapes. And if you ever come into my store asking for grapes again, I will nail your webbed feet to the floor, do you get me?"

So the duck leaves. A week goes by and finally the duck comes back. He waddles up to the counter and asks the man, "Do you have any nails?"

"Sorry, pal," says the man. "Sold out."

"Good," says the duck. "Do you have any grapes?"

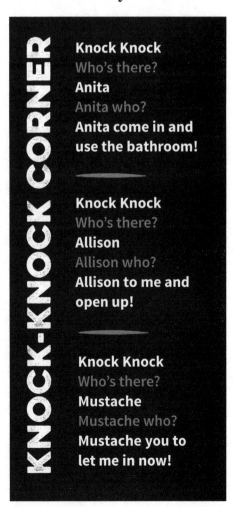

KNOCK-KNOCK CORNER

Knock Knock
Who's there?
Anita
Anita who?
Anita come in and use the bathroom!

———

Knock Knock
Who's there?
Allison
Allison who?
Allison to me and open up!

———

Knock Knock
Who's there?
Mustache
Mustache who?
Mustache you to let me in now!

SHAGGY DOG STORIES

A LAWYER wakes up in the hospital after a terrible car accident. When he realizes what happened, he begins to sob hysterically.

"My Mercedes!" he cries. "My beautiful Mercedes is totalled!!"

The doctor at his bedside shakes his head and scolds the lawyer.

"You are so materialistic!" he says. "Did you even realize that you lost your left arm??"

The lawyer looks at where his arm used to be and begins to cry even harder.

"My Rolex!!"

A MAN is sitting on a bench waiting for a bus when another man sits next to him, sighing dejectedly.

"What's wrong, buddy?" the first man asks.

The second man puts his face in his hands and begins to sob hysterically.

"It's my wife," he says. "She kicked me out of the house and told me not to come back or even speak to her for a month."

"Gee, pal," the first man says. "I'm real sorry to hear that."

"I know," the second man says. "The month is up today."

A LION is sitting on the Serengeti when suddenly a gorilla runs up and slaps him across the face.

The lion roars and tears off after the gorilla. The gorilla runs until he finds a campsite. He throws on a khaki shirt, a khaki vest, a pith helmet and a pair of glasses. Then he sits down by the fire with a cup of coffee, opens up the newspaper and pretends to read. Just then the lion bursts into the camp roaring angrily.

"Grrr, did you see a gorilla come through here?" he asks.

The gorilla puts down the paper and looks over his glasses.

"You mean the one who slapped a lion in the face?"

"Oh man!" says the lion. "It's in the paper already??"

SHAGGY DOG STORIES

A ZOO WORKER is driving a flock of penguins to the zoo when suddenly he has a blowout and lands in a ditch. The penguins get out and are wandering all over the road. As the zoo worker tries to herd them back into the truck, he sees another car coming down the road. He frantically flags it down.

"Can you help me?" he asks the driver. "I need you to take these penguins to the zoo."

"Sure thing," the driver says. "Pile 'em in!"

The driver and the zoo workers get the penguins in the car and he drives off. A few hours later, the zoo worker is on his way to the zoo when he suddenly sees the driver coming from the other direction with the penguins still in the car. He waves his arms, trying to get him to stop. The driver stops and rolls down his window.

"What the heck are you doing?" the zoo worker asks. "I told you to take those penguins to the zoo!"

"I did!" says the driver. "Now we're going to the movies."

A COWBOY goes to a stable looking for a new horse.

"Well," says the stable master. "Wish I could help you, but the only one we got is this old nag. He's kind of stubborn. The only way to make him stop is to yell 'Hey, hey, hey!' Just like that. Three times. And then the only way to get him to go again is to yell 'Thank God!'"

"OK," says the cowboy. "Sounds easy enough. I'll take him."

So the cowboy takes the horse and they go riding off

through the desert at full speed. Eventually, the cowboy spots a cliff right up ahead. In a panic, he struggles to remember the command to stop the horse.

"Ho, ho, ho!" he yells. The horse doesn't stop.

"Hi, hi, hi!" he tries. Again no luck.

"Hee, hee, hee!" he screams, but the horse keeps going.

Now the cliff is only inches away. At last, the cowboy remembers the right command.

"Hey, hey, hey!" he yells. The horse stops suddenly right at the edge of the cliff.

"Oh!" the cowboy says, relieved. "Thank God!!"

Duke dons dapper attire, date unknown.

John Wayne and
Lee Marvin in the
1963 John Ford film
Donovan's Reef.

FUNNY FILM
DONOVAN'S REEF

JOHN WAYNE'S 1963 ISLAND COMEDY WOULD SERVE AS A FITTING FAREWELL TO THE CAMARADERIE HE SHARED WITH DIRECTOR JOHN FORD OVER THE YEARS.

In July of 1962, John Wayne would fly to the Hawaiian island of Kauai to begin production on what would be the final film he'd make with his mentor, the legendary director John Ford. The setting for several of his previous films as well as the venue for his wedding to wife Pilar, Hawaii was a home away from home for Duke at this point; and the addition of Ford made the work environment even more comfortable. Though

111

the collaborative duo had developed a reputation for their fun-loving antics behind the scenes, the films they made were largely no-nonsense, gritty affairs. But this time, with *Donovan's Reef*, John Wayne and John Ford were finally able to let the good times roll on the big screen as well.

Filled with knee-slapping quips and side-splitting slapstick, *Donovan's Reef* pays perfect homage to the mischief the legend and his closest pals were known for on set. Though Ward Bond, the third member of their troublemaking trio, was no longer around to join Duke and Ford in their cinematic sendoff, the director found a way to immortalize the uniquely physical camaraderie the late actor shared with John Wayne. The film features Duke in the believable role of Michael Patrick "Guns" Donovan, a World War II hero now serving as the affable owner of Donovan's Reef, a saloon on the tranquil Polynesian island of Haleakaloha. Each year on December 7, however, Donovan and his war buddy Thomas Aloysius "Boats" Gilhooley (Lee Marvin) disturb the peace by engaging in an amusing yet unorthodox holiday tradition: a knock-down-drag-out bar brawl. As the two punch each other onto pianos, upturn tables and crash into a slot machine, it seems anything goes in the friendly fist fight—that is, until Gilhooley picks up a brown bottle and prepares to throw. "Not the brandy, you dope!" Donovan yells. "Sorry!" Gilhooley replies as he gently places the bottle back onto the bar before resuming his mission to knock his pal loopy.

Much of the film's comedy comes from the quarreling, will-they-or-won't-they relationship between Donovan and Amelia Dedham (Elizabeth Allen), the estranged daughter of Donovan's other war buddy, Doc Dedham (Jack Warden). Arriving on the island in hopes of exposing her father's reckless lifestyle in order to overtake the family shipping line, the Boston-bred Amelia threatens the carefree vibe Donovan has established in Haleakaloha— but that doesn't stop him from having fun at her expense. When Donovan begrudgingly takes Amelia waterskiing, she shows off by egging him on to drive the boat faster, to which he gleefully obliges until she crashes face-first into the water. Undeterred back on the boat, Amelia challenges Donovan to a swimming race back to shore before stripping off her heavy, wet attire to reveal a skimpy swimsuit underneath. As he

in yachting cap and dungarees, is no different from Mr. Wayne at ease with a 10-gallon hat and six-shooters. He is still as massive as a moose." Recognizing Duke and Ford's intent to make something reflective of their straight-shooting, laugh-filled friendship, *The New York Herald Tribune* critic Judith Crist noted the film's "complete lack

"YEAH, WELL, FRANGIPANI AND FLAME-THROWERS DON'T SEEM TO GO TOGETHER, BUT THAT'S THE WAY IT WAS." —DONOVAN

stares, Donovan stammers, "Let's uh, let's go...." Sure enough, the bickering duo eventually embrace their blossoming feelings for one another—though their squabbling shows no signs of stopping.

In the eyes of critics, Duke's larger-than-life presence and innate charisma were in no way diminished by the less serious role of Michael Patrick "Guns" Donovan. Following the release of *Donovan's Reef, The New York Times* wrote, "Mr. Wayne,

of pretension when it comes to the purity of corn or the exploitation of a cliché." Putting it more succinctly later in her review, Crist dubbed the film "good, clean, simple-minded fun," something of which the director and star certainly knew the value. The rough and rowdy relationship John Wayne and John Ford built over their many years working together may have met its conclusion, but *Donovan's Reef* allows it to live on in all its good-natured glory.

113

Lauren Bacall and John Wayne on the set of *The Shootist* (1976).

"I LIKE BEING IN A GOOD PERSONAL STORY. I DON'T CARE IF I'M SITTING IN AN ARMCHAIR, STANDING ON TOP OF A BUILDING OR JUMPING OFF OF IT— IF IT'S JUMPING OFF OF IT, I DON'T DO IT ANYWAY."

—Behind-the-scenes footage from *The Shootist* (1976)

SHAGGY DOG STORIES

A MAN is driving along a country road when his car breaks down in front of a farm. The farmer agrees to fix the man's car, saying that it will take a few hours. The man walks around the farm, taking in the sights, and notices a three-legged pig walking around the pen. When the farmer comes by to tell him his car is ready, the man decides to ask him about it.

"So," he says, "what's the story with the three-legged pig over there?"

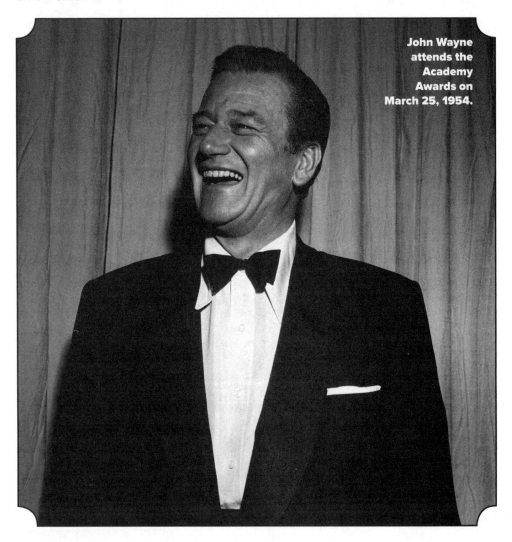

John Wayne attends the Academy Awards on March 25, 1954.

"That pig?" the farmer asks. "Let me tell you about that pig. One night, my family and I were sleeping and the house caught fire. That pig oinked and oinked until we woke up and then, not only did he lead us safely out of the house, but he went back in to rescue our dog!"

"Wow," the man says. "That is some pig."

"You don't know the half of it," the farmer says. "Last winter, I fell through the ice down at Egan's Pond. And that pig raced out onto the ice and pulled me out of the water."

"You've got to be kidding," says the man.

"And just last week," the farmer went on, "our house was being robbed and this pig tackled a burglar and stood on him oinking away until we woke up and could call the cops."

"That is amazing," says the man. "So why does he have three legs?"

"Well," the farmer says. "A pig that good, you don't eat him all at once!"

A MAN and his dog are waiting at a talent agent's office. The agent calls them in and is already unimpressed.

"Look, pal," says the agent. "I've seen a lot of dog acts and they're all terrible. So unless you've got something really amazing for me, let's just call it a day, OK?"

"No, no," the man says. "Trust me! This is going to blow your mind. This here is Floinker the Wonder Hound. And she is a legitimate, one hundred percent real talking dog. Are you ready?"

"Fine," the agent says. "Let's see what you've got."

"OK," he says. "Floinker, what would you say if you sat on sandpaper?"

Floinker says, "Ruff! Ruff!"

"Great!" the man says. "Now, tell me, what is on the top of a house?"

Floinker wags her tail and says, "Roof! Roof!"

"Good girl!" says the man. "Last question, who is the greatest baseball player of all time?"

Floinker leaps up and down and says, "Ruth! Ruth!"

The agent angrily throws the two of them out of his office, screaming at them for wasting his time. Out on the street, Floinker looks up at her owner.

"OK, OK, you were right," she says. "I should have said Ty Cobb!"

THREE EXPLORERS are preparing a trek through the desert. On the morning they are about to leave, they review the items they plan to bring on the trip. The first explorer says, "I've packed plenty of canteens so we'll never be short on water!"

The second explorer says, "I brought a tent so we'll be protected from the elements while we are sleeping at night!"

The third explorer holds up a car door.

"What did you bring that for?" the other explorers ask.

"It gets hot in the desert," the explorer says. "This way, we can roll down the window!"

TWO PIONEERS are exploring the wilderness in search of a route to the sea, when suddenly they come across a bear. They quickly scramble up a pine tree and try to wait him out, but the bear is hungry and doesn't leave. After an hour, the two pioneers realize the bear isn't going anywhere. The first one looks at the other.

"Okay," he says. "Here's what we're going to do. Let's jump down and make a run for it."

"You really think I can outrun a bear?" asks the other pioneer.

"Normally I'd say you have a 50/50 shot," says the first pioneer. "But since I'm 100 percent certain I can outrun you, I think the odds are a little skewed..."

A NEW RECRUIT arrives for duty on board an aircraft carrier. He is overwhelmed by the sheer size of the ship, finding it to be almost like a small floating city. It takes him some time just to find his way to his bunk. After a day on the ship, he suddenly feels a very urgent call

KNOCK-KNOCK CORNER

Knock Knock
Who's there?
Annie
Annie who?
Annie chance you might let me in?

Knock Knock
Who's there?
A little old lady
A little old lady who?
I didn't know you could yodel!

Knock Knock
Who's there?
Ice cream
Ice cream who?
Ice cream until you let me in!

of nature. Frantic, he runs around, looking everywhere for a bathroom, but to no avail. Finally, he comes across another sailor and stops him in the hallway.

"Shipmate!" he says. "Can you help me find the head?"

"That's on the port side," the other sailor says.

"Port?" the new sailor screams frantically. "That's three weeks away!"

A YOUNG BOY goes to visit his grandfather for the weekend. When he sits down for breakfast, he notices that the plates look dirty.

"Pop pop?" the boy asks. "Are these plates clean?"

"Why of course they are, my boy!" says the grandfather. "They're as clean as water can get them."

This seems to satisfy the boy and they eat breakfast. When lunchtime comes around, again, the boy notices that the plates don't seem to be as clean as they could be.

"Pop pop?" the boy says. "I don't want to be rude, but are you sure these plates are clean?"

"Now what did I say?" the grandfather says. "They're as clean as water can get them!"

Dinner time rolls around and again the plates don't look clean.

"Pop pop," the boy says. "I really don't think that these plates are clean."

"Listen here boy," said the grandfather. "I don't know how many ways I gotta say it! These plates are as clean as water can get them!"

Lucille Ball, John Wayne and Vivian Vance on *I Love Lucy*.

Just then the dog jumps up on the table and the grandfather immediately scolds him.

"Get down, Water! Good boy."

A WEALTHY MAN is walking down the street when a homeless man approaches him.

"Hey mac," the homeless man says. "You got any change?"

"I do not have any money to give you," says the wealthy man. "But I will offer you a job."

"Hey, that's great!" the homeless man says. "What do

you need?"

"Come to my house tomorrow morning," the wealthy man says. "I will leave paint out front for you. Paint my porch for me and then ring the bell when you're done and I will pay you."

"You got it, mac!" says the homeless man.

At the end of the following day, the wealthy man's doorbell rings. He opens the door and finds the homeless man standing there covered in bright blue paint and holding a roller.

"All done, mac!" he says. "Except, you don't have a Porsche. You have a Ferrari!"

A MAN comes home to find a note on his son's bed. He picks it up and reads it, horrified at what it says:

Dear Dad,

I have decided to run off and elope with Brenda, the neighbor's daughter. I know we are both only 17, but our love cannot be denied. Also, she is pregnant and the baby is mine. We are going to live in a trailer park and get jobs working at the bowling alley.

Sweat beading on the father's brow, his hands begin to shake as he continues reading...

With a year of hard work, I can probably work my way up to spraying shoes or even setting up the pins. I'm sure you're worried about money, but please don't. Brenda and I are going to make some cash by doing a few breaking and entering jobs for her uncle—he helped us hock your suits and mom's jewelry so we'd have enough for a nest egg to get us started. It's not much, and we know things will be tough, but like you always say: "Love conquers all!"

Your loving son,
Mike

PS: None of this is true. I just wanted to remind you that there are worse things than what's on the report card in the kitchen!

THREE GUYS are sitting in a lobby about to be interviewed for a job. The first guy goes in and notices that the boss does not have any ears.

The boss says, "This is a job that requires tremendous powers of observation. Make an observation about me."

"That's easy," the first guy says. "You don't have any ears!"

The boss immediately becomes enraged. "Get out!" he yells.

The second guy goes in and again the boss asks that he make an observation about him.

"Ummmm," says the second guy. "You've got no ears?"

The boss again becomes irate and angrily throws the second guy out of his office. The guy stands up, dusts himself off and walks over to the third guy.

"Look pal," he says. "Whatever you say in the interview, don't mention the fact that the boss doesn't have any ears. It's obviously a sore subject. Got it?

Don't mention the ears!"

"Got it," says the third guy as he goes in for the interview.

"Now," says the boss as the third guy sits down. "As I told the other applicants, this is a job that requires tremendous powers of observation. Make an observation about me."

The third guy studies the boss a moment and then says, "You wear contacts!"

"Excellent!" says the boss. "An astute observation and not an easy one to make. I am impressed. Tell me, how did you know that I wear contacts?"

"Well," says the third guy. "How could you wear glasses? You don't have any ears!"

TWO PARATROOPERS were about to jump out of a plane. One turns to the other and says, "What's the secret to keeping your job here?" The other paratrooper points to his parachute.

"It's all about pulling the right strings."

A NAVAL OFFICER walks into a club and orders something to quench his thirst.

"It's been a long deployment," he tells his host. "I've been out at sea for a month. And you know what got me through? Marine jokes. Day in, day out, nothing but

Marine jokes. You want to hear one?"

The host fixes the Naval officer with a hard stare and says, "Now listen, before you tell me that joke, I want to tell you something. You see the bouncer at the door? He's a Marine. And the guy at the end of the bar with the muscles and the mean look? He's a Marine too. And right now you're looking at the meanest, toughest Marine ever to shoulder a rifle. So, now that you know that, let me ask you: You sure you want to tell that joke?"

"Well," says the Naval officer, "not if I have to tell it three times!"

John Wayne on the set of *The Alamo* (1960).

John Wayne
on the set of
the 1976 film
The Shootist.

"FOR A MILLION DOLLARS...THAT AND I KINDA LIKE BEING BUFFALO BILL."

—When asked on *The Phil Donahue Show* why he grew a mustache

SHAGGY DOG STORIES

A NAVY RECRUIT reports for his first day at boot camp and is approached by a commander.

"Son," says the commander. "Do you know how to swim?"

"Why?" asked the recruit. "Don't you have ships?"

A YOUNG SAILOR sits down in the galley for his first meal on a submarine.

"How's the food?" he asks a fellow sailor.

The sailor shrugs. "Sub-standard."

A MAN comes home late after a long day at work. He throws his keys on the table, goes to the fridge and grabs a bottle of water. He then goes to the oven to warm up his dinner and, when he opens the door, there is a raccoon curled up inside. He jumps back, startled.

"Hey! What do you think you're doing in my oven?" he yells at the raccoon.

The raccoon looks at the man in confusion.

"Is this a Westinghouse?" the raccoon asks.

The man takes a brand of the oven and nods, "Yes it is" to the raccoon.

"Then pwease cwose the door." the racoon says. "I'm twying to west!"

TWO MARINES are conducting a training exercise using paintball guns. Out of nowhere, one Marine shoots the other, emptying his paintball clip.

"Why did you shoot me?" the other Marine asks.

The first Marine shrugs.

"Just to watch you '*dye.*'"

A MAN is in a butcher shop when he sees a dog walk in carrying a piece of paper in his mouth. The butcher takes the paper and reads it over. He then proceeds to slice a quarter pound of roast beef, a pound of turkey and a half-pound of swiss cheese for the dog. The dog then reaches into a little pouch on his collar, pulls out the proper amount of money, pays for the cold cuts and barks twice as if to say "Thank you!" He then takes the cold cuts in his mouth and turns to leave the butcher shop. On the way out, he runs smack dab into the door. He looks back sheepishly at the man and the butcher, then uses his paw to pull the door open and walks out of the butcher shop. The butcher watches him go and then turns to the man.

"That dog is so stupid," he says.

"What do you mean?" the man replies. "That was really impressive!"

"Impressive?" the butcher says. "That's the third time he's been here this week and he still can't remember he has to pull the door open!"

Foreground from left:
Kenneth Tobey and John
Wayne in *The Wings of
Eagles* (1957).

SIDE-SPLITTING SCENES

EVEN IN SOME OF HIS FILMS THAT AREN'T CONSIDERED COMEDIES, JOHN WAYNE WAS ABLE TO ELICIT BIG LAUGHS.

BIG BREAKFAST FOR THE BADMAN

As its title suggests, 1947's *Angel and the Badman* digs deep into the extreme contrast between its main characters, Duke's gunslinging outlaw Quirt Evans and Gail Russell's prairie Quaker girl Penelope Worth, who rescues and cares for Quirt after he's left for dead. The dynamic between the two is immediately amusing when Quirt wakes from unconsciousness in the home of Penelope's family and doesn't hesitate to indulge his appetite for the most important meal of the day. When asked if he'd like two or three eggs for breakfast, the gunman requests six; and after scarfing down a feast befitting a larger-than-life legend such as Duke, the charming Quirt quips, "Funny thing about pancakes: I lose my appetite for 'em after the first couple o' dozen."

SINK OR SWIM

In a memorable scene from 1953's *Hondo*, John Wayne's titular Army dispatch rider provides a youngster with an invaluable lesson. When Hondo Lane approaches 6-year-old Johnny Lowe (Lee Aaker), son of Geraldine Page's Angie Lowe, who is fishing at a pond, he offers the boy some advice: "Always fish with the sun in your face." But when Hondo hears Johnny reveal that he can't swim, he realizes there's a much more urgent lesson to be taught. "You can't what?!" he asks in disbelief as he leans down to the boy's level. After hearing "I can't swim" from Johnny a second time, Hondo, without saying another word,

swats the fishing pole out of the young man's hand, scoops him up and tosses him right into the pond. As Johnny frantically flounders, Hondo yells out, "Just reach out in front of you and grab a handful of water, pull it back towards you." The boy soon makes it to shore, full of pride as he exclaims, "I did it!" putting a celebratory stamp on a scene that continues to crack up viewers today.

UNIFORMED FOOD FIGHT

Portraying the real-life flier and friend of director John Ford, Duke balances heartbreak with humor as the inspiring Frank W. "Spig" Wead in *The Wings of Eagles* (1957). In a scene depicting a joint celebration with the Navy and Army, Wead makes a good-natured jab at the Army's commanding officer, claiming the Navy "won't need more than a kite to beat you" in a race around the world. "Why don't you fly this!" the officer retorts as he shoves a piece of cake in Wead's face, much to the delight of his fellow men in green. Not to be outdone, Wead dumps the entire cake on the commanding officer's head, thanks the rest of the troops for the party and initiates a slapstick slugfest that provides some earned levity in the classic film.

ELEPHANTS KNOW NO BOUNDARIES

When he stepped into the role of Sean Mercer, a big game catcher exploring Africa in 1962's *Hatari!*, John Wayne reminded audiences why he could never

trunks. Later, the elephants even visit the reunited Sean and Dallas in the bedroom, collapsing the bed in the process.

QUICKFIRE COMPETITION

The charismatic cowboys played by Duke and Kirk Douglas in *The War Wagon* (1967) naturally attract trouble everywhere they go— but that doesn't stop them from

LOMAX: "MINE HIT THE GROUND FIRST." TAW: "MINE WAS TALLER." — *THE WAR WAGON* (1967)

quite be pigeonholed. Packed with snappy dialogue, push-and-pull romance and a bevy of wild African animals throughout, the film hits its humorous high point just before the credits roll. Upon realizing he can no longer suppress his true feelings for Dallas (Elsa Martinelli), Sean employs baby elephants to help him track her down. Finally, they find Dallas in a convenience store, which of course results in the adorable mammals excitedly trampling displays and knocking down shelves with their

having a little fun along the way. On their way to steal gold from a nefarious miner, the two men are momentarily sidetracked when a couple of outlaws attempt a sneak attack. Always ready for action, Taw (John Wayne) and Lomax (Kirk Douglas) simultaneously spin around and shoot down their foolish fouls in one fell swoop. "Mine hit the ground first," Lomax quickly points out. "Mine was taller," Taw responds, adding a dose of repartee to the already indelible scene.

John Wayne and Barbara Streisand at the 42nd Academy Awards.

"IF I'D HAVE KNOWN THAT, I'D HAVE PUT THAT PATCH ON 35 YEARS EARLIER."

—Suggesting the eyepatch he wore in *True Grit* (1969) was key to finally winning the Academy Award for Best Actor

A FEW FOR THE ROAD

John Wayne in *The Undefeated* (1969).

ALRIGHT, PILGRIM, BEFORE YOU HIT THE TRAIL, SADDLE UP WITH A FEW OF THESE CLASSIC "DAD" JOKES.

WHEN is a cat not telling the truth?
When he's a lion

DID YOU HEAR about the man who drowned at the chocolate factory?
Mourners say he was the sweetest man in town.

HOW CAN you call up an oyster?
On a shell *phone*

WHAT DO you call a train full of dentists?
The Molar *Express*

DID YOU HEAR about the dolphin who splashed water at the people on shore?
It seems he did it on porpoise.

WHY DID the melons get married in a church?
Because they cantaloupe

Wild Goose captain Bert Minshall and John Wayne.

"I SHOULD BE PAID A PERFORMING FEE!"

—said to Bert Minshall regarding the *Wild Goose* captain's frequent filming of home movies aboard the boat

A FEW FOR THE ROAD

WHY DID the writer stop using his unsharpened pencil?
It was pointless.

WHAT HAPPENED to the frog who parked in a handicapped space?
His car was toad.

HOW DID the leopard change spots?
He moved.

WHY DIDN'T the pizza maker like pizza jokes?
They were too cheesy.

WHY CAN'T you trust an atom?
They make up everything.

WHY DIDN'T the lobster ever share?
He was very shellfish.

WHAT'S brown and sticky?
A stick

WHY DID the man go off the all-almond diet?
It was too nuts.

HOW DO YOU make a tissue dance?
Just put a little boogie *in it*

WHAT HAPPENED to the customer who discovered how bad his electrician was?
He was shocked.

DID YOU SEE how I hung up that picture?
Nailed it

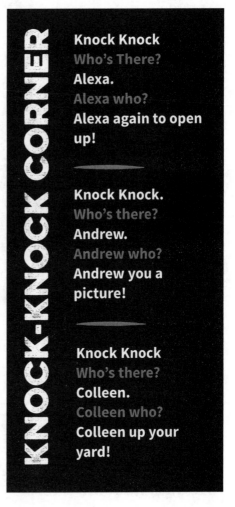

KNOCK-KNOCK CORNER

Knock Knock
Who's There?
Alexa.
Alexa who?
Alexa again to open up!

Knock Knock.
Who's there?
Andrew.
Andrew who?
Andrew you a picture!

Knock Knock
Who's there?
Colleen.
Colleen who?
Colleen up your yard!

John Wayne on the set of *The Alamo* (1960).

WHERE DO fish keep their money?
A river bank

WHY COULDN'T the dog open a bookstore?
He only had one tale.

WHAT HAPPENS to a seagull when it flies over the bay?
It becomes a bay-gull.

WHY ARE bats always happy?
They just eat anything that bugs *them.*

WHY DID the math book go see a psychiatrist?
It had too many problems.

HOW CAN YOU play piano in bed?
Use sheet *music*

I'D LIKE TO die in my sleep like my grandfather.
Not awake and screaming like his passengers

WHO WAS happiest when the *Titanic* sank?
The lobsters in the galley

A FEW FOR THE ROAD

WHAT HAPPENED to the man who broke his arm in two places?
  He stopped going to those places.

———

WHY DID the man never report his credit card stolen?
  The thief still spent less than his daughter.

———

WHY WAS the duck sent to the mental institution?
  He quacked *up.*

———

WHAT DO YOU CALL a fly with no wings?
  A walk

———

WHERE SHOULD YOU take a cow on a first date?
  To the moo-vies

———

WHAT DOES Sir Lancelot become when he has insomnia?
  A sleepless knight

Duke poses with fans on the set of *The Alamo* (1960).

WHAT'S the favorite video game platform in France?
Wii

WHY COULD the teacher only name 25 letters of the alphabet?
He didn't know Y.

John Wayne at the 42nd Academy Awards.

"I'M AN AMERICAN MOVIE ACTOR, I WORK WITH MY CLOTHES ON. I HAVE TO. HORSES ARE ROUGH ON YOUR LEGS. AND ON YOUR ELSEWHERES."

—On stage at the 42nd Academy Awards

A FEW FOR THE ROAD

WHAT HAPPENED when the past, present and future all met up?
It was a tense situation.

DID YOU HEAR about the guy who got a brain transplant?
He was looking for someone to change his mind.

DID YOU HEAR about the model who loved to use a taser?
She was a real stunner!

WHY DIDN'T the man ever look for his lost watch?
He couldn't find the time.

WHY DO golfers carry around extra pairs of pants?
In case they have a hole in one

WHY IS IT POINTLESS to push the envelope?
No matter how much you push, it's still stationery.

WHY DID THE MAN find a wooden shoe in the toliet?
It was clogged.

=====

HOW DO YOU overcome your fear of walls?
You've got to get over it.

=====

WHY ARE dead batteries a good deal?
They're free of charge.

=====

WHAT DID the man say to his X-ray technician?
"You can always see right through me."

=====

WHAT DID his fellow mathematicians say to the guy who invented the zero?
"Well, thanks for nothing!"

=====

WHAT DID the husband say to his wife when she wanted them to become vegetarians?
"That's a big 'missed steak!'"

A FEW FOR THE ROAD

HOW DID the doctor treat his patients' kleptomania?
He told him to take something for it.

WHAT KIND of songs do you write about tortillas?
Wrap *music*

WHY DO YOU have to be careful working out underwater?
You don't want to pull a mussel.

WHAT DO YOU get when you treat your cows too well?
Spoiled milk

WHY DID the man get fired from the calendar factory?
He took a day off.

KNOCK-KNOCK CORNER

Knock Knock
Who's there?
Fillmore
Fillmore who?
I'd Fillmore confident if you knew who I was!

Knock Knock
Who's there?
Gus
Gus who?
Gus you'll never know!

Knock Knock
Who's there?
Hugo.
Hugo who?
Hugo to the door and find out!

DID YOU HEAR about the kidnapping at school?
Don't worry, he woke up.

WHY DIDN'T the couple go to the German sausage restaurant for their anniversary?
They knew it'd be the wurst.

WHY DID the coffee go to the police?
It kept getting mugged.

WHAT'S THE SECRET to making a good egg roll?
Just push it down a hill.

DID YOU HEAR about the cheese factory that exploded?
They're still sifting through de brie.

WHERE DO YOU find a turtle with no legs?
Wherever you left him

Don Rickles and
John Wayne on
*The Don Rickles
Show*, c. 1975.

"PLEASE, NOT TOO MUCH APPLAUSE— THIS IS AN OLD BUILDING."

—Greeting the audience of *The Don Rickles Show*

John Wayne and Goldie Hawn on an episode of *Rowan & Martin's Laugh-in*, September 11, 1972.

SMALL SCREEN, BIG LAUGHS

DUKE'S APPEARANCES ON VARIETY TV OVER THE YEARS HAD VIEWERS DOUBLING OVER IN THEIR LIVING ROOMS.

T hough he spent decades developing the no-nonsense persona he became beloved for on the big screen, John Wayne was always willing to set his seriousness aside when the opportunity came along. And for a major movie star of the mid-20th century, television—particularly variety shows—often provided such an opportunity. Duke's willingness to poke fun at his own image made him a must-have guest on many popular programs; and half a century later, the laughs he elicited still resonate.

THE COLGATE COMEDY HOUR
John Wayne made his variety television debut on the October 1953 edition of *The Colgate Comedy Hour*, one of the greatest forebearers of the format. The episode saw the icon joining host Jimmy Durante in a skit in which the two take turns singing, trading quips and fumbling lines. At one point, the sketch even veered into

meta territory when Durante asked Duke, "Who's got the next line, you or me?" drawing big laughs from the crowd as well as John Wayne himself.

THE MILTON BERLE SHOW

Shortly after his successful stint on *The Colgate Comedy Hour*, John Wayne stopped by *The Milton Berle Show*. The Western star insisted to the host and the audience that unlike other movie stars who make TV appearances, he was not there to shamelessly promote a film. The statement turned out to be a setup for a brilliant bit in which Duke turned around to reveal a flashing sign attached to his pants that read "HONDO."

THE JACK BENNY PROGRAM

In 1960, John Wayne would drop by *The Jack Benny Program* for an episode titled "John Wayne Show." A recurring bit sees the comedy legend host double-booking himself for dinner with his guests, which leads to Duke volunteering to take violinist Jaye P. Morgan out on the town instead. When Duke and Morgan arrive at the restaurant, they see Benny moonlighting as a tableside violinist.

THE DEAN MARTIN SHOW

The release of 1965's *The Sons of Katie Elder* was the perfect time for John Wayne to stop by his co-star and close friend Dean Martin's variety show. The two entertainment icons of the era put their comedic chemistry on full display as Martin talked Duke into "singing" the show's theme song "Everybody Loves Somebody Sometime." The bit became apparent as the tune began to play and John Wayne opened his mouth, clearly lip syncing to Martin's pre-recorded vocals. In 1966, Duke would return to *The Dean Martin Show* for a segment in which he and Dino sat on horses and chewed the fat. When John Wayne complimented his occasional co-star for never missing a line when they shot films together, Martin joked that the horse he rode in Westerns was Mr. Ed, who delivered the lines on his behalf.

THE GLEN CAMPBELL GOODTIME HOUR

On the September 14, 1971, episode of *The Glen Campbell Goodtime Hour*, the host entered the set on horseback to tell the audience about his experience working with John Wayne in *True Grit* (1969). After saying he really looked up to Duke because the star "had the biggest darn horse you ever saw," Campbell flipped the script and brought the legend out on a considerably smaller steed. The two then discussed John Wayne's iconic film career, with the star quipping "the good ones" began with *Stagecoach* (1939) and noting he still had bad dreams about playing a singing cowboy in the 1933 B-Western *Riders of Destiny*.

THE BOB HOPE SHOW

With comedic chemistry dating back to their days performing for troops overseas as part of the USO Camp Shows, John Wayne and Bob Hope created lasting laughs together when Duke swung by *The Bob Hope Show* in November of 1971. In a sketch styled after the hit series *All in the Family*, John Wayne played the conservative sheriff father to Hope's young liberal character. Considering the host was actually four years older than Duke, the casting alone was plenty amusing.

ROWAN & MARTIN'S LAUGH-IN

Between the years of 1968 and 1973, John Wayne would become a near staple of variety television by appearing in a total of 14 episodes of *Rowan & Martin's Laugh-In*. It was

during this run that viewers at home got to see Duke like they'd never seen him before: in a bunny suit. But that's not all. In one of his most memorable moments on the show, John Wayne joined Kent McCord, Martin Milner, Charles Nelson Reilly, Ed Asner, Glenn Ford, Redd Foxx, Jack Carter, Ernest Borgnine and Howard Cosell in singing a purposely poor rendition of "Row, Row, Row Your Boat" as part of a "Hollywood Boys Glee Club."

THE DON RICKLES SHOW

In his final variety show appearance, Duke would go out in style by yukking it up with one of the most beloved comedians of all-time, Don Rickles. On the January 1975 episode of *The Don Rickles Show*, the host claimed his guest wanted to be brought out "anonymously" to spare himself in the event that his jokes didn't land. Donning a Lone Ranger mask, the mystery guest—who was clearly John Wayne—made his way onto the stage. Sure enough, Duke's legitimate confidence quickly took over as he removed the mask and began rattling off jokes. "Please, not too much applause," the legend quipped to the crowd "This is an old building."

A FEW FOR THE ROAD

WHY WAS the chef a tough boss?
He'd always beat the eggs.

WHY WERE sodium chloride and sulphuric acid in jail?
For a salt and battery

DID YOU HEAR about the new movie *The Elevator*?
It works on so many levels.

I HEARD Arnold Schwarzenegger won't be playing the Terminator anymore.
I guess he's an ex-Terminator.

WHAT'S THE best way to have a good day at work?
Go home

WHY CAN'T you be too sad on Sunday?
Because the day before is always a sadder-day.

WHY CAN'T dogs get MRIs?
Because it's a CAT *scan*

―――――――

HOW DID the Eskimo fix his broken house?
Igloo'd it *[he glued it]*

―――――――

DID YOU HEAR about the woman who spent her whole life looking for a perfect match?
She eventually used a lighter.

―――――――

WHY ARE fire engines red?
Because they're always rushin'

―――――――

WHAT DID the husband do when his wife told him he had no sense of direction?
He packed up and right.

―――――――

WHAT'S THE recipe for holy water?
Just boil the hell out of it.

A FEW FOR THE ROAD

WHAT WAS the kindergartner accused of when he refused to take a nap?
Resisting a rest

HOW DID the astronaut enjoy the book he was reading in zero gravity?
He found it hard to put down.

HOW MUCH is pie in Jamaica?
Sorry, I don't know the pie rates of the Caribbean.

HOW DOES a one-armed man climb a ladder?
Single-handedly

DID YOU HEAR about the felons who were arrested for tearing a calendar in half?
They got six months each.

WHY DID the fireman wear red suspenders?
He was sloppy with the ketchup.

John Wayne and Richard Widmark on the set of *The Alamo* (1960).

WHEN IS the best time to go to the dentist?
Tooth-hurty

THERE'S A RUMOR going around about peanut butter...
But I won't spread it

161

John Wayne on
the set of *Rowan &
Martin's Laugh-in*,
c. 1972.

"I CAN OUT-HOP ANYONE WITH ONE EAR TIED BEHIND MY BACK!"

—Wearing a bunny costume on *Rowan & Martin's Laugh-in*

A FEW FOR THE ROAD

WHAT DID the orchestra conductor name his twin daughters?
Anna One, Anna Two...

=====

WHAT DID one ice cream cone say to the other?
"I'll never dessert *you."*

=====

AN UNCLE was put in charge of naming his brothers' kids. He named the girl Denise. What did he name the boy?
De-nephew

=====

WHAT HAPPENS when boiled water leaves a tea kettle?
It will be mist.

=====

WHY GO to the barber just to get a haircut?
Shouldn't you get them all cut?

=====

DID YOU HEAR about the guy whose whole life was about the Hokey Pokey?
Eventually he turned himself around.

DID YOU HEAR about the two vegans who made up with each other?

They had no beef.

WHY DIDN'T the man go to work after being run over?

He was tired.

WHY ARE all vacuum cleaners so useless?

All they do is gather dust.

WHY WAS the lettuce so embarrassed?

He saw the salad dressing.

DID YOU HEAR about the guy who wrote a book on bears?

Paper would have been easier.

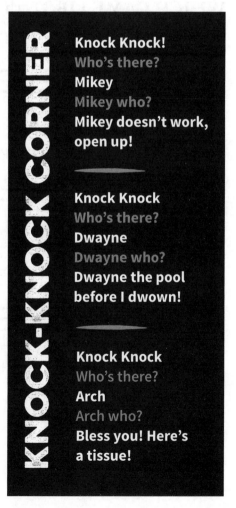

KNOCK-KNOCK CORNER

Knock Knock!
Who's there?
Mikey
Mikey who?
Mikey doesn't work, open up!

Knock Knock
Who's there?
Dwayne
Dwayne who?
Dwayne the pool before I dwown!

Knock Knock
Who's there?
Arch
Arch who?
Bless you! Here's a tissue!

A FEW FOR THE ROAD

WHERE DO PEOPLE go to learn to make ice cream?
Sundae *school*

HOW COME French fries aren't French?
They're cooked in Greece.

WHICH CAME FIRST, the chicken or the egg?
Order them online and then wait and see.

WHY IS BEING a chef a tough job?
Sometimes the work can get a bit whisky.

WHAT DO YOU NEED to give someone sailing to Hawaii?
A Pacific *set of instructions*

HOW DID the lawyer get the picture cleared of all charges?
He proved it was framed.

CAN A kangaroo jump higher than a house?
Yes. Houses can't jump at all.

WHAT IS a sea monster's favorite meal?
Fish and ships

WHERE DOES an otter keep its money?
In a river bank

WHY WOULD a fish make a terrible musical instrument?
You can tune a guitar, but you can't tuna fish.

WHY ARE dogs such bad storytellers?
They only have one tail.

WHAT DID THE GUY do when his wife asked him to sync her phone?
He threw it in the lake.

John Wayne and
Dean Martin on
*The Dean Martin
Show*, c. 1965.

"DEAN, I CAN'T TELL YOU HOW HAPPY IT MAKES ME TO SEE YOU STANDING ANYWHERE!"

—On *The Dean Martin Show*

John Wayne and his daughter Marisa at a USC Celebrity Baseball Game on April 17, 1977, in Los Angeles, California.

KIDDING
THE
KIDS

JOHN WAYNE'S CHILDREN WERE THE BEST AUDIENCE—AND OCCASIONALLY THE BEST SUBJECTS—FOR HIS GOOD-NATURED HUMOR.

When a man becomes a father, he seems to acquire a special skill for comedy that can either have his children rolling on the floor or rolling their eyes (especially once those kids become teenagers). Being an entertainment icon with a knack for timing and plenty of charisma to boot, John Wayne was undoubtedly a bit more gifted than the average Joe in the art of dad humor.

KIDDING THE KIDS

Plus, as the father of seven children, Duke was fortunate to have plenty of ears to test his material out on.

"Sometimes you'd be the object of a joke, but it was always an expression of affection," the star's son Patrick Wayne says. As the third-eldest of John Wayne's children, Patrick was able to avoid much of his father's ribbing and instead laugh along as one of his younger siblings endured some Duke humor. Recalling an anecdote in which his father's ability to play it straight helped him land an amusing bit on the family boat, he says, "Once when my youngest sister was on the *Wild Goose*, she had these decals, and my dad took one of them and stuck it on the side of the ship. He called her over and said, 'Aissa, what is the meaning of this?' pointing to the decal. He played this out for a while until she was almost in tears but then we all had a big laugh about it."

As great an asset as it was for providing his kids with comedic relief, Duke's deadpan delivery could sometimes be mistaken for dead-seriousness.

In an interview with *AARP*, the icon's daughter Melinda Wayne recalled a now-amusing misunderstanding that occurred when she and her brothers and sisters traveled to Ireland to stay with their father while he filmed *The Quiet Man* (1952): "As we got off the plane in Shannon, he said, 'I know you're going to want to buy gifts and take stuff home, but you've got to earn the money.' So at 10 years old, I was thinking, 'Oh my God, I've got to get a job!'" The following morning, the young go-getter walked all around the Irish town until she was able to convince a shop owner to let her sweep the floors. When she returned home, she found her family in a panic—except for Duke. "My dad was sitting at the dining room table, very calm, and he said, 'Nice of you to show up for breakfast. Where have you been?'" Melinda remembered. Once his daughter revealed she'd actually gone and gotten a job, Duke wasn't quite as calm. "He said: 'You what? I meant here! On the set! To be in the crowd scenes!'"

John Wayne sometimes

even saw his own misfortune as the perfect opportunity to bring a little lightheartedness to his children's lives. As the Hollywood hero's youngest daughter Marisa Wayne once told *AARP*, her first time golfing with her father yielded both a scary experience and an amusing moniker that would

Blood was coming out of the side of his head. And down he went. Whump! A couple of men got an ambulance," Marisa remembered.

When John Wayne regained consciousness in the hospital, he asked to see Marisa right away. Being so young and uncertain in the situation, the

---

"SOMETIMES YOU'D BE THE OBJECT OF A JOKE, BUT IT WAS ALWAYS AN EXPRESSION OF AFFECTION."

---

stick with her. "We went out to a driving range, and I'm swinging and swinging and missing the ball," Marisa said. "He came around and said, 'Honey, just watch the ball and make contact.' I swung the club and the ball was still there—but I could tell I made contact with something." That "something" Marisa's club made contact with was Duke's personal, skull-shaped hat rack. "I turned around and saw my father staggering around.

star's daughter naturally feared she was about to be in serious trouble. But sure enough, upon seeing the youngster who had just cracked a golf club against his head, Duke seized the moment to crack a joke. "I went in there, and all he said was, 'Well, you're the only one who had the nerve to do this to me!'" Marisa remembered. From that day forward, he called her by a nickname that commemorated the slapstick incident: "Nine Iron."

John Wayne and Victor McLaglen on the set of *Fort Apache* (1948).

"I DON'T AVOID OVEREATING AT LUNCH."

—When asked by *Variety* how he avoids overeating at lunch on a film set

Media Lab Books
For inquiries, call 646-838-6637

Copyright 2021 Topix Media Lab

Published by Topix Media Lab
14 Wall Street, Suite 4B
New York, NY 10005

Printed in Canada

ISBN-13: 978-1-948174-73-2
ISBN-10: 1-948174-73-1

CEO Tony Romando

Vice President & Publisher Phil Sexton
Senior Vice President of Sales & New Markets Tom Mifsud
Vice President of Retail Sales & Logistics Linda Greenblatt
Director of Finance Vandana Patel
Manufacturing Director Nancy Puskuldjian
Financial Analyst Matthew Quinn
Digital Marketing & Strategy Manager Elyse Gregov

Chief Content Officer Jeff Ashworth
Director of Editorial Operations Courtney Kerrigan
Creative Director Steven Charny
Photo Director Dave Weiss
Executive Editor Tim Baker

Content Editor Trevor Courneen
Art Director Susan Dazzo
Designer Kelsey Payne
Associate Editor Juliana Sharaf
Copy Editor & Fact Checker Tara Sherman

JOHN WAYNE
ENTERPRISES

Topix Media Lab would like to thank John Wayne Enterprises, custodian of the John Wayne Archives, for providing unfettered access to their private and personal collection. Best efforts were made by Topix Media Lab to find and credit the photographers.

Topix Media Lab makes no specific claim of ownership of images contained in this publication and is claiming no specific copyright to images used. The mission of the John Wayne Cancer Foundation is to bring courage, strength and grit to the fight against cancer. *www.johnwayne.org*